MICHEL FOKINE

MICHEL FOKINE

(From the bronze by Isamo Nahuchi)

MICHEL FOKINE
& HIS BALLETS

By

CYRIL W. BEAUMONT

ILLUSTRATED

* *
*

LONDON

DANCE BOOKS
15 Cecil Court, London WC2N 4EZ

First published in 1935

Reprinted in 1996 by Dance Books Ltd
15 Cecil Court, London WC2N 4EZ

ISBN 1 85273 050 1

A CIP catalogue record of this book
is available from the British Library

Printed in Great Britain by
BPC Wheatons, Exeter, Devon

To

MICHEL FOKINE

In Friendship and Admiration

PREFACE TO FIRST EDITION

THIS book is an attempt to record the choregraphic achievements of Michel Fokine from 1905 to 1925, in which connection I desire to express my sincere appreciation of his kindness in so patiently answering all my enquiries.

In the course of my text I have dealt but briefly with Fokine's plans for the reform of the ballet, since he himself has set down his views at length. These essays will be found in Appendix A, to which I have added the admirable *Dialogue with Fokine* compiled by Dr. Pierre Tugal, Keeper of the Archives Internationales de la Danse, Paris, to whom I am indebted for so courteously permitting me to translate and publish this work.

Fokine's more recent activities will be found summarised in Appendix C.

All dates referring to performances given in Russia are in the " old style," and are therefore thirteen days behind our own calendar.

C. W. B.

PREFACE TO SECOND EDITION

THIS book, which has long been out of print, is now reprinted in response to numerous requests. Ten years have passed since this study first appeared, an interval which has witnessed many Fokine revivals for various ballet companies, of his best known compositions, also the production of several important new works such as *Don Juan*, *L'Epreuve d'Amour*, *Paganini*, and *Bluebeard.* Finally, to the great loss of the world of the Dance, the famous choreographer passed away at New York on the 22nd August, 1942.

After much cogitation I have decided to leave my book as written and not attempt to bring it up-to-date. Those of my readers, however, who seek information regarding Fokine's ballets of the last decade will find full accounts of them in my *Complete Book of Ballets* and in the *Supplement* to that volume.

CYRIL W. BEAUMONT.

CONTENTS

ILLUSTRATIONS

ILLUSTRATIONS

CHAPTER ONE

FIRST STEPS

I

MICHEL[1] MIKHAYLOVICH FOKINE was born at St. Petersburg on the 26th of April, 1880. Neither of his parents was connected with the stage, his father being a well-to-do man of business. The future choreographer was the youngest of five children—four boys and a girl. In order of age they were Vladimir, Sophia, Nicholas, Alexander, and Michel. Of the sons, Nicholas was an officer in a cavalry regiment, Vladimir became a dramatic artiste well known for his rendering of comedy parts, while Alexander became the director of the Troitsky Theatre which specialised in miniature plays and farces, a form of entertainment with which Londoners are familiar through the visits of Baliev's Theatre of the Chauve Souris, and the Blue Bird Company directed by Yuzhny.

Fokine, like many another famous dancer, manifested at an early age a disposition for the dance. While other children played at being soldiers, coachmen, or wild animals, he was always endeavouring to express his high spirits in lively movements, an inclination which was continually fostered in him by his soldier brother who, a constant source of inspiration and guidance to him in his early years, encouraged and strengthened him no less when in after times he was oppressed by doubt and disappointment at the obstacles he experienced, in his first efforts to direct the art of ballet into an entirely new channel.

Nicholas, though much attached to his profession, was profoundly interested in the arts ; he passed his leisure hours in visits to art galleries, reading the best authors

[1] Michael is, of course, the exact English equivalent of Mikhayl, but, as M. Fokine prefers the French form, Michel, and invariably employs it when not writing in Russian, we have used this style throughout.

and studying history. It is he who dominates Fokine's memories of his early years.

Although the Fokines lived at St. Petersburg, they also had a summer residence on the Krestovsky Ostrov. There the boys led an outdoor life and indulged in many riverside sports. The family belonged to a yacht club and among the members was another family, whose little girl was a student at the Imperial School of Ballet. This girl was a great friend of Michel's sister, Sophia, and when the Fokines returned to St. Petersburg the friendship continued.

One day Sophia, accompanied by her brother, Nicholas, went to the School of Ballet to visit her friend. They returned home enraptured with all they had seen. For the benefit of their brothers they imitated the dancers' steps and poses and, thereafter, playing at ballet was their favourite game. This amusement fostered a real interest in ballet, and, as Michel's gracefulness on these occasions had often been remarked, there was talk of having him trained as a dancer. While his mother was in favour of the plan, his father was strongly opposed to it. There was considerable argument, but in the end the father gave way.

When Fokine was nine years old his mother applied for him to be admitted to the Imperial Ballet School attached to the Maryinsky Theatre at St. Petersburg. He passed the preliminary examination in the rudiments of reading, writing, and arithmetic, and the doctors and *maîtres de ballet* having approved of his physique, he was accepted as a daily pupil.[1] He began to learn his first steps in the preparatory class conducted by Platon Karsavin, the father of the future *ballerina*, Thamar Karsavina. The new pupil made rapid progress and the next year, late in 1890, was transferred to the senior class conducted by the same professor, taken as a boarder, and granted exemption from payment.

In 1891, having now studied with Karsavin for two years, Fokine was promoted to the next class presided over by Volkov. This professor's teaching was dull

---

[1] There were 100 applicants of whom eight were accepted.

12

MICHEL FOKINE IN THE " RIBBON DANCE "

[*Photo: K. A. Fischer, St. Petersburg*

MICHEL FOKINE AS LUCIEN D'HERVILLY
IN " PAQUITA "

and pedantic, but he had one great merit. He was a strict disciplinarian, and would never permit a pupil to take an incorrect position or execute a step carelessly ; and every movement had to be executed with mathematical precision. He suppressed all originality and never took the slightest pains to develop a pupil's individuality, preferring to drum into every member of his class a wonderful sense of exactitude. He never said that a certain movement could be performed in this manner or that, for him there was one method only, and having once detailed it he would not permit the deviation from it by a hair's breadth. However exasperating this may have been at the time, in later years, when Fokine essayed the composition of ballets, he found this sense of precision instilled into him by Volkov of the utmost value.

From time to time Fokine was permitted to dance in the school *corps de ballet*, and at the age of eleven he appeared in the annual Pupils' Display, which was held according to tradition in the small theatre attached to the School for the Theatre. These performances were important events in the life of the pupils, and were invariably honoured by the presence of the Tsar. The monarch present on this occasion was Alexander III, while the ballet written for this production was *The Magic Flute* (music by Drigo, choregraphy by L. I. Ivanov). Ivanov, who had remarked the technical skill and expressiveness of Fokine's dancing at the examinations, entrusted him with the principal part of the peasant Lucca, in which, despite his youth, he achieved a great success.

II

From his first years at school Fokine surprised everyone with his unusual and varied talents, and revealed a particular aptitude for dancing, mime, music, and painting. At the same time, an unusual trait for one of his early years, he borrowed from the school library quantities of books on art and the theatre, which he read with avidity. At twelve years old he went to see Shakespeare's plays performed at the Alexandrovsky Theatre, and visited

13

the Hermitage and other galleries to study Russian and foreign art. He became deeply interested in Shakespeare, and from then onwards began to study the works of Gervinus relating to that author, and also Russian and foreign literature dealing with the same subject.

Volkov died some months after Fokine had joined his class, and his place was taken by Shirayev with whom he studied until 1893, when he was transferred to the highest class conducted by P. A. Gerdt. The latter was perhaps the best teacher Fokine ever had. His character and importance have been so well stated by Svetlov that we reproduce his words : " Gerdt, for a long period, was the pride and essence of our ballet. For beauty of figure and gesture, for distinction of manner or stage expression, no other dancer could equal him. His dramatic powers were a true inspiration, besides being extraordinarily varied. His academic dancing was exceptional in its nobility, while his consummate art of mime produced everywhere the deepest impression.[1]"

In character Gerdt was the exact opposite to Volkov, being good-natured and easy-going with the pupils. He cared little for technical explanations or the analysis of steps. He demonstrated a step, and the boys did their best to imitate his movements. Gerdt resigned in 1896, when his place was taken by N. Legat, with whom Fokine continued his studies.

In 1898 Fokine passed his final examination (held on this occasion, according to the advice of the professors attached to the school, not in the small school theatre, but at the Mikhaylovsky Theatre) with such success that the examiners, headed by M. I. Petipa and P. A. Gerdt, drew up a petition which they forwarded to I. A. Vsevelojsky, the Director of the Schools for the Theatre, requesting him to take Fokine into the ballet company in view of his outstanding talents and value to the theatre. The petition was granted, and Fokine was at once cast for important parts, notwithstanding the rule that every artiste must begin his career in the *corps de ballet*. Another

[1] *Thamar Karsavina*, 1922.

14

point of interest is that while the customary salary for a newly-fledged artiste was 50 r. per month, Fokine, however, was allotted a monthly salary of 66 r. 66 k., an increase which serves as an additional proof that he was already regarded as a dancer of promise.

III

Fokine made his *début* on the stage of the Maryinsky Theatre on the 26th of April, 1898, when he appeared with Egorova, Syedova, and Obukhov, in the *pas de quatre* in *Paquita* (music by Deldevèze, choreography by Mazilier).

He then joined the special class for artistes conducted by Christian Petrovitch Johannsen, a Scandinavian professor who had been a pupil of Bournonville, the *maître de ballet* who contributed so much to the development of the Danish ballet. Johannsen, like Volkov, was a pedant. His class was an academy of classical ballet, a school of choreographic counterpoint. His aim was the development of technique, insistence on the strictest correctitude in the positions of the head, arms, feet, legs, and body; the preservation of strength and precision. His intention, however, was not to fetter the dancer with academic laws, but to provide him with a secure foundation for later individual expression.

At this period he was a very old man and rarely rose from his chair, where he sat with his violin resting on his knees. Now and again he would take up the instrument, play a few bars, *pizzicato*, and explain with beautifully expressive hands the movements that must accompany the music. The pupils would gather about him and watch with loving interest the steps indicated by his long, tapering fingers, which they would strive to perform. Then the old professor would correct them, requesting one leg to be lowered, another to be bent, an arm to be raised or more rounded, and the head to be turned in this direction or that. Perhaps his greatest asset was his wonderful knowledge of the academic dance. In his long and varied career he had danced with many of the greatest dancers of the past; he had known the work

15

of the most famous choreographers of his day. His brain was an encyclopædia of the best traditions of classical ballet, and for his lessons he daily drew from this inexhaustible storehouse some new steps to give to his pupils.

In 1902 Fokine was appointed to teach the technique of the classical ballet to the class for junior girls. He gave his lessons every morning from nine to twelve. The pupils were divided into two classes : one from nine to ten-thirty, the other from ten-thirty to twelve.

He worked whole-heartedly at these lessons, so that often they lasted beyond the time-table set by the authorities, a proceeding which brought upon him severe reprimands. In 1905 he was promoted to direct the senior class.

As this work is primarily concerned with Fokine's contribution to the art of choregraphy, we shall not deal with his career as a dancer, a subject which requires a whole study to itself. Fokine, however, was a fine mime and an excellent dancer, strong yet graceful, and full of expression and style-atmosphere, a view which cannot but be endorsed by all those who had the good fortune to see him dance in the early years of the Diaghilev Company. But, long before that, he had achieved a considerable reputation as a dancer. He was Pavlova's first partner in Russia with whom he appeared in *Arlequinade* at the Maryinsky Theatre, and that is to mention only one of the many celebrities with whom he danced. Pavlova loved to work with him and took the principal parts in most of his early ballets.

ANNA PAVLOVA AND MICHEL FOKINE IN "ARLEQUINADE"

[*Photo : K. A. Fischer, St. Petersburg*

SCENE FROM " DON QUICHOTTE," MOSCOW PRODUCTION

[*Photo : K. A. Fischer, St. Petersburg*

SCENE FROM " LE LAC DES CYGNES," MOSCOW PRODUCTION

TYPICAL LATE NINETEENTH CENTURY GROUPS. DEVISED
BY THE MOSCOW CHOREGRAPHER, ALEXANDER GORSKY

CHAPTER TWO

THE IMPERIAL RUSSIAN BALLET UNDER PETIPA

I

TO realise the conditions under which Fokine began his training and the obstacles he had to overcome in order to introduce his reforms, which, in their eventual achievement, produced as great an evolution in the then obtaining ideals of choregraphic art as those effected by Noverre in those of his epoch, the reader must be acquainted with the principles instituted by Petipa—a name which is perhaps the greatest in the history of the classical ballet and which stands for a period covering a whole half-century of plastic art.

Marius Petipa was born at Marseille on the 11th of March, 1822 ; his father was a dancer, his mother a tragic actress. In 1840 he made his *début* in a principal part at the Comédie Française, when he danced with Carlotta Grisi at a performance held for the benefit of the celebrated actress Rachel. He then went to Bordeaux and afterwards toured Spain. In 1846 he danced at the Paris Opera with Fanny Elssler.

In 1847 he accepted an offer to fill the post of *premier danseur* to the St. Petersburg branch of the Imperial Russian Ballet—rendered vacant by the departure of Emile Gredlu —at which city he arrived on the 24th of May. He made his *début* in *Paquita* and in 1858 produced his first independent ballet called *Un Mariage au Temps de la Régence*. But it was not until four years later that he was appointed *maître de ballet* in recognition of his having composed in the short space of six weeks a long ballet called *La Fille de Pharaon*, which achieved a considerable success.

Petipa exerted a remarkable influence on the classical ballet of the last half of the nineteenth century. One of his contributions was an incessant and unswerving effort to develop technique. He demanded from his principals the highest standard of execution and insisted that the young dancers training in the schools should be fitted to take their place. Italian dancers possessed of extraordinary technique, such as Virginia Zucchi and Pierrina Legnani —famous for her thirty-two *fouettés*—were added to the company, and the continual raising of the technical standard, the constant incentive given to competition, caused dancing to tend to transgress the boundary line of acrobatics.

It must not be thought, however, that Petipa was favourably disposed towards an *acrobatic* technique, for, in fact, contrary to the majority of the *maîtres de ballet* of his time, he admired most the classical traditions of the French school of which he himself was a fine example. The truth is that he only fought half-heartedly against the invasion of the Italian dancers and even allowed acrobatic " numbers " to be introduced into his own productions.

Mme. Karsavina has described the Petipa ballets as follows :

" At the outset of my career, Marius Petipa was coming to the end of his profession as *maître de ballet*. He had had a long experience and had done much useful service to choregraphy. He had a remarkable command of mass on the stage and sometimes the form taken by his *ballabiles* showed considerable imagination. But his productions were all founded on the same formula. An inevitable *divertissement* brought his ballets to an ever happy conclusion ; while such of his heroes for whom anything but a tragic end was an historical impossibility found themselves crowned in a final apotheosis. His ballets tended to be ' *féeries.*' In his later years he made some attempts to modernise his art to accord more nearly with the present time, but he never felt at ease when making these efforts and they were unsuccessful. His ballets, which even now have not disappeared from the repertory of the Maryinsky Theatre, were crowded with marches and processions which often interrupted, without any kind of logical excuse, long continuous scenes of pantomine and beautifully composed dances."[1]

Petipa was a very methodical worker who planned out his ballets stage by stage, making copious notes and sketching the arrangement of the " groups " before he called a rehearsal. Although he had composed twelve ballets prior to his Russian engagement, he learned a great deal respecting choregraphic composition from the famous Jules Perrot, who was *maître de ballet* at St. Petersburg in

[1] " *Souvenirs d'Enfance.*" *Musica*, Dec., 1912.

1847 and remained in that post for twelve years. Perrot was very interested in the young dancer and frequently selected him for his assistant when producing new ballets.

Petipa possessed an almost Napoleonic capacity for work. New *variations, pas de deux, pas de trois, ballabiles,* poured from him like water from a running fountain, and he rarely repeated himself. Those who saw the revival of *La Belle au Bois Dormant* (*The Sleeping Princess*) at the Alhambra Theatre in 1922, or have seen the excerpts from it which have been, and are still being, given from time to time in London, will have a good idea of the technical beauty of his compositions.

A full record of his achievements presents a catalogue of almost incredible labour. He controlled the Russian ballet for over fifty years, during which time he composed 54 new ballets (generally of four or five acts, and often containing seven or eight scenes), reconstructed 17 old ones, and supplied the dances for 35 operas. He died in July, 1910.

In Petipa's time, custom and tradition reigned supreme. No ballet was composed as the result of collaboration between librettist, composer, *maître de ballet*, and decorative artist. Everyone worked independently, shut up, as it were, in his own office, until music, dances, costumes, and scenery were complete, when the whole was assembled with results that sometimes were far from satisfactory.

II

Let us consider the production of a ballet at this period. The author of the theme, who frequently had little acquaintance with either music, choreography, or painting, selected a legend or story which he happened on by chance and which took his fancy. This he transposed into a ballet, dividing the action over five or six acts, regardless of whether the interest was sufficiently strong to warrant such treatment.

The sole requisite for success was that everything should centre on one principal character to be interpreted by the *prima ballerina ;* for the slightest incident, the feeblest action, served as excuse for bringing in a dance.

There never existed a stranger world than that imagined by the writers of ballet *scenarii*; the course of history was completely changed, the inhabitants common to one land were transported thousands of miles to a place for which their physical characteristics and dress totally unfitted them, rivers which geography has stated to be in Russia and Spain found themselves in Egypt. Never was there such a topsy-turvy world, unimagined by the greatest of romancers.

Next, a composer was instructed to write the necessary music. There must be so many dances, so many marches in this act, so many in that. In general, the dances were composed to familiar, easy rhythms like the polka, mazurka, or waltz. If the ballet were Spanish the melodies recalled well-known national airs seasoned with the indispensable castanets : if Russian, the composer turned to a Russian folk dance, and so on. If no particular style were specified, a good waltz, march, or polka was certain to ensure success. And since it often happened that the composer was little acquainted with the *scenario*, the music sometimes afforded a ludicrous contrast to the action of the piece.

The *maître de ballet* worked, again independently, on the dances. Everything was governed by rule. The *prima ballerina* must have her *pas de deux* with its *variations* and *coda*, while the ballet must contain at least one *pas d'action* for the dancer to display her miming abilities. Then there must be a *variation* for the *premier danseur* and *ballabiles* for the *corps de ballet* to give the principals time to rest and change. Lastly it was necessary to devise opportunities for the processions in which a crowd of supers marched and counter-marched like soldiers in geometrical figures, finally to form in a mass to serve as a background for the *ballerina* to display her technique.

The scene-painter also worked by himself. He had a competent knowledge of historic ornament and the styles of architecture characteristic of different epochs, but his work was lifeless, devoid of style-atmosphere, and in-artistic. In short, the setting rarely harmonised with the spirit of the ballet. On the other hand it must be admitted that there was little encouragement for a real artist

EGYPTIAN　　　　　　　GYPSY

POLISH　　　　　　　GREEK (?)

SOME TYPICAL COSTUMES FOR BALLET, LATE 19TH CENTURY

(Note especially the contemporary coiffures and jewellery worn by the dancers)

[*Photo: K. A. Fischer, St. Petersburg*

MICHEL FOKINE AS JAIN DE BRIEN
IN " RAYMONDA "

to design artistic scenery, because there was no demand for it.

The costume-designer proceeded in like manner. The foundation of all dresses was the ballet skirt, pink *maillot*, and rose-coloured ballet-shoes. If the dress were to be Greek, a Greek key pattern was added to the edge of the skirt; if Egyptian, a lotus flower; if German, that was conveyed by the addition of a dark velvet bodice, a small silk apron, and a few bands of red ribbon sewn to the edge of the skirt; if Polish, a few pieces of gold or silver braid were stitched horizontally across the bodice in Hussar fashion and the edges of the sleeves and skirt tipped with fur. The dancer's *coiffure* followed the prevailing fashion, whatever character was interpreted, and was often decorated with a diamond crescent or tiara. *Balletomanes* saw nothing incongruous in this, or nothing strange in that a dancer interpreting a humble slave should wear jewelled bracelets and pearl necklaces.

If the *ballerina* were satisfied with her dances, well and good; if not, it was easy to cut the offending numbers, regardless of whether the musical sequence was interrupted or not. Again, there were few scruples at borrowing favourite numbers of proved success from old ballets in order that the *ballerina* should repeat her former triumphs; the possibility that they might not accord with the new production was immaterial.

Such, then, was the position of affairs which Fokine, acting in obedience to some inner impulse, felt himself called upon to reform.

CHAPTER THREE

FIRST ESSAYS IN CHOREGRAPHY

I

AS Fokine pursued his studies he became more and more convinced that there were many fixed customs in the ballet routine which needed elucidation. He was convinced that ballet had reached a point beyond which it could not advance so long as it continued to be bound by the iron rules of tradition. Clearly the technique of the pure classic ballet had been developed to the last degree, but he felt that it was artistically wrong to employ it for the choreographic expression of every theme. In his opinion there was confusion where there should be homogeneity, and he sought enlightenment from his teachers and questioned them.

"Why," he asked, "in an Egyptian ballet were the dancers in ballet costume and the supers in the dress of the period? Why did a certain dancer execute such and such difficult steps, what were they intended to express, for surely if dancing were not expressive it became acrobatic, mechanical, and meaningless? Why in ballet was a psychological feeling always expressed by a fixed gesture or series of gestures which neither described nor symbolised anything? Why must the arms be always rounded, the elbows always held sideways parallel to the audience, the back straight and the feet always turned out with the heels to the front? Why was ballet technique limited to the movement of the lower limbs and a few conventional positions of the arms, when the whole body should be expressive to the last muscle? Why did a dancer rise *sur les pointes* not to convey the impression that she was rising from the ground, but in order to astonish the audience with their strength and endurance? Why was the style of a dance always inharmonious with that of the theme, its costume, and its period?" But to each question he received the stereotyped answer: "Because it is tradition."

Fokine pondered deeply and came to the conclusion that if the art of ballet were to be lifted out of the rut in which it was embedded, it must be freed of the conventional costume and gestures, and the set order of steps ; technique must be employed as a means and not as an end ; and finally, there must be unity of action and unity of style in accordance with the music used, which should be expressive.

In 1904, Fokine happened to read the " *Daphnis and Chloe* " of Longus. On this he based the *scenario* for a two-act ballet which he submitted to the director of the Imperial Theatres with explanatory notes regarding the production of the piece. These notes included a plan for the reform of ballet.

The following extracts will make clear the wealth of perception and logic displayed by this young man of twenty-one :

The dance need not be a mere *divertissement*, introduced into the pantomime. In the ballet the whole meaning of the story can be expressed by the dance. Above all, dancing should be interpretative. It should not degenerate into mere gymnastics. It should, in fact, be the plastic word. The dance should explain the spirit of the actors in the spectacle. More than that, it should express the whole epoch to which the subject of the ballet belongs.

For such interpretative dancing the music must be equally inspired. In place of the old-time waltzes, polkas, pizzicati, and galops, it is necessary to create a form of music which expresses the same emotion as that which inspires the movements of the dancer. The harmony which these dances must have with the theme, the period, and the style, demands a new view-point in the matter of decoration and costume. One no longer demands the eternal short skirts, pink tights, and satin ballet-shoes. One can give way to the freedom of artistic fantasy.

The ballet must no longer be made up of " numbers," " entries," and so forth. It must show artistic unity of conception. The action of the ballet must never be interrupted to allow the *danseuse* to respond to the applause of the public.

In place of the traditional dualism, the ballet must have complete unity of expression, a unity which is made up of a harmonious blending of the three elements—music, painting, and plastic art.

The great, the outstanding, feature of the new ballet is that in place of acrobatic tricks designed to attract applause, and formal entrances and pauses made solely for effect, there shall be but one thing—the aspiration for beauty.

Through the rhythms of the body the ballet can find expression for ideas, sentiments, emotions. The dance bears the same relation to gesture that poetry bears to prose. Dancing is the poetry of motion.

Just as life differs in different epochs, and gestures differ among human beings, so the dance which expresses life must vary. The Egyptian of the time of the Pharaohs was different from the marquis of the eighteenth century. The ardent Spaniard and the phlegmatic dweller in the north not only speak different languages, but use different gestures. These are not invented. They are created by life itself.

The only outcome of this labour of love was the issuing of an order to the effect that, in view of the necessity for preserving the illusion and theatrical impression, artistes were forbidden to bow during the performance of an *opera*. Evidently the management considered the preservation of illusion in ballet of no importance.

II

On the 10th of April, 1905, Fokine made his first essay in ballet composition when at the annual Pupils' Display he reproduced *Acis et Galatée*. This ballet, with music by Kadletz, had been given some years previously with choregraphy by Ivanov. It was a Greek ballet which Fokine wished to revive with movements in the Greek style.

He went to the St. Petersburg Public Library in search of suitable material but, on asking the librarian if he had any good books on Greek art, was told that such volumes were not on the ordinary shelves and that he had better consult the director. He was received very pleasantly by M. Stassov, who greeted him with the words : " You are the first artiste of the ballet to come here. We have the most wonderful material, yet no one ever troubles to come and examine it." This ballet was an experiment limited to improvising Greek movements on ballet technique, for Fokine felt the impossibility of trying to stage a ballet in pure Greek style when the dancers' training was limited to the traditional methods.

The ballet included a faun dance by boys, one of whom was Nijinsky. The dancers did not wear traditional costumes and so Fokine was able to compose freely. This dance, in fact, was the first sketch for a future composition, the Venusberg ballet in *Tannhauser*, given some five years later. Although *Acis et Galatée* was only an experiment, it contained an element of fantasy then quite unknown.

ANNA PAVLOVA AND MICHEL FOKINE

ANNA PAVLOVA IN "LE CYGNE"

From the statuette by Rosalès

The well-known producer A. Sanine was so delighted with Fokine's first effort that he begged the management to permit Fokine to arrange the dances in a new piece he was producing. But as Fokine was not officially a *maître de ballet*, the request was refused. Sanine was greatly annoyed, resigned from the service of the Imperial Theatres, and wrote a letter to the press. This letter was the first to proclaim Fokine a *maître de ballet*.

Enthusiastic over the possibilities of ballet reform, Fokine next composed a letter which he sent to various artistes asking them to favour him with their views on ballet. What did they understand by ballet ? What was the future of ballet ? Some artistes did not trouble to reply, while others appeared to hold no particular views on the subject.

It is not difficult to realise the extent of Fokine's disappointment when he found that not only did the general public refuse to take the ballet seriously, but even the artistes themselves appeared to regard it purely as a means of existence. He began to wonder whether it was worth while to devote his life to an art held in such little honour, a doubt which was strengthened by the fact that he was making progress in the art of painting. Again, his father had never looked kindly on his wish to enter the Theatre School, saying : " I do not want my Mimotchka to become a jumping-jack." Nevertheless, Fokine felt so strongly the possibility of speedy success and of being able to reform the ballet that he decided to continue.

III

The same year was marked by the production of the dance now known all over the world as " *Le Cygne* " (" *The Dying Swan* "). The dancer Anna Pavlova visited the rehearsal-room and told Fokine that she had promised to appear at a concert to be given at the Hall of the Assembly of Noblemen by the artistes of the chorus of the Imperial Russian Opera, and asked him to arrange a dance for her. Fokine consented and then considered what form the dance should take. He mused on the dancer's long and graceful neck, the softness of her line, and felt that the dance should be beautiful, lyric, and expressive. *Le Cygne* was born from those thoughts.

Not only is this dance one of Fokine's most beautiful and poetic creations, but it illustrates to the full his conceptions of the art of ballet, and is based on the traditional costume and technique of the old ballet. This dance demands in the dancer a high standard of technique which, however, is not used to astonish but to create a poetic image—the symbol of the everlasting struggle between life and death. The execution is not limited to the movements of the lower limbs ; the whole body from head to toe is important. " *The Dying Swan* " is not merely an appeal to the eye of the spectator, but an appeal to his innermost thoughts. The dance symbol is emphasised by the charm of the costume, the hair framed in a fillet of white feathers, and the skirt adorned with little touches of swansdown. The music is by C. Saint-Saëns.

No one who has not seen this dance can imagine the impression it produces on the mind and heart of the spectator. The pitiful fluttering of the arms, the slow sinking of the body, the pathetic eyes, and that final pose when all is stilled, arouse an emotion so deep and so overwhelming that some moments elapse before the spectator can voice his appreciation by means of applause.

I

THE next year (1906), on the 20th of March, Fokine composed another ballet for the Pupils' Display. This
was *A Midsummer Night's Dream*, arranged to Mendelssohn's composition and an adagio from the same composer's
Violin Concerto. There were a number of elves (Nijinsky
was the principal) who danced against a background of
girls posed like garlands of flowers in opposition to the
arm-groupings in the style of the traditional ballet.

Soon afterwards, Fokine was invited by the artistes of
the Maryinsky Theatre to produce a ballet in aid of the
"Gogol Society." And on the 8th of April he staged
La Vigne (The Vine), a ballet in three acts composed by
Anton Rubinstein which had been written for some special
occasion but not performed, owing to difficulties and
unsuitabilities in the music. The parts were taken by
dancers of high reputation like Bekefi and Marie Petipa,
promising young artistes such as Vera Fokina, Thamar
Karsavina, Lydia Kyasht, and Anna Pavlova, and Fokine
himself. It was the first time the young choreographer had
composed with artistes of the Imperial Theatre and he
was somewhat troubled at having to teach those whom,
from his childhood, he had been accustomed to look upon
as celebrities.

The scene showed a dark cellar filled with casks of wine.
People in old-fashioned dresses entered the cellar and
broached the casks one after the other, which afforded
opportunities for dances representative of the qualities of
the different wines the casks contained. The visitors
drank the wine and the ballet ended in a final orgy. The
performance was a brilliant success. Among the distinguished audience was Marius Petipa, who showed his
approval by sending Fokine a warm message of congratula-
tion: "*Cher Camarade, enchanté de votre composition,*

27

continuez et vous serez un grand maître de ballet." This little
note was dearer to Fokine than all the floral tributes and
compliments which he received even in his early
productions.

II

The succeeding year, 1907, was marked by two important
productions, *Eunice*, and *The Animated Gobelins.* The first,
staged on the 10th of February in the cause of charity, was
given at the invitation of M. Dandré for the benefit of
the " Society for the Protection of Small Children." Fokine
found some interesting music by Stcherbatchev to which
he adapted a theme based on one of the episodes in
Sienkiewicz's *Quo Vadis ?*

This ballet was composed with a *plastique* derived from
a study of the paintings on Greek vases. It was conceived
in the style of the antique processional dance and revealed
the poetry and beauty resident in the human form which
the old ballet had disregarded. The dancers were clad in
Greek *chitons*, but since, at this period, the use of bare
legs and feet on the stage would have been considered
indecent, Fokine compromised by letting his dancers wear
maillot with a suggestion of toes. Some artistes wore
sandals in addition. The ballet included a " Torch Dance "
by the *corps de ballet*, and an Egyptian Dance performed
by Syedova, Rutkovskaya, and Obuklova, with four boys
dressed as Nubians. The latter was the first sketch for
one of the dances in a later production : *Une Nuit
d'Egypte.* There were no false gestures, the attitudes
being taken from figures in Egyptian sculpture.

During the rehearsals, Fokine was visited by the celebrated *balletomane*, Besobrasov, who told him that in his
endeavour to accomplish something new, he was going
too far, that he wished to change everything, do away with
ballet-shoes, and eliminate dancing *sur les pointes.* He
suggested that while the *corps de ballet* might be dressed
in Egyptian costume, he should let the principals wear the
traditional ballet-skirt. But Fokine was not to be turned
from the path he had determined to follow, and told the

balletomane that he felt his conception would be spoilt if he mixed two opposed styles and that he would not be cast down if his effort failed.

Eunice, despite its inequalities as a connecting-link between the old ballet and the new, created a feeling of deep astonishment. For the first time in the history of the Russian ballet, artistes clad in Greek costume danced a Greek ballet in the Greek style[1]. The mimed drama was explained by expressive movements, instead of the old conventional gestures. The principal parts of Eunice, Acté, and Petronius were interpreted respectively by M. Kschesinskaya, A. Pavlova, and P. A. Gerdt. The applause was most enthusiastic. *Eunice* was repeated the next season when the roles of Eunice and Acté were taken by Pavlova and Karsavina respectively.

II

The Animated Gobelins was staged on the 15th of April in connection with the annual Pupils' Display. Fokine had to arrange a ballet for his pupils but could not decide what to produce. As usual he had to find something either quite new, or else so old as to have been forgotten. While at a concert he heard a piece entitled *Suite from " Le Pavillon d'Armide,"* by N. Tcherepnine. He was charmed by the music, and, having learned that the composer was present, went to speak with him. They were introduced and Tcherepnine was much pleased at his wish to produce the piece as a ballet, even though it was for a pupils' performance. He explained that the theme was

---

[1] It has been stated that Fokine's reforms were inspired by Isadora Duncan. But this dancer did not visit St. Petersburg until 1907, and Fokine's plan for ballet reform had already been submitted to the directorate of the Imperial Theatres in 1904. There was undoubtedly a similarity of aim in their common demand for naturalness, expressiveness, and simplicity ; but their methods of attaining these ideals were diametrically opposed. Duncan's dancing was free, Fokine's compositions were stylisations imposed on dancers trained in the technique of the classical ballet. Admittedly, certain of the dances in Fokine's ballets on Greek themes bore an element of resemblance with some of the movements and poses in Duncan's dances, but that was simply because they both sought inspiration from the same source—the art of ancient Greece.

suggested by the painter Alexander Benois and intended for a ballet in three acts, although at present he had composed only the music for one scene, that entitled *The Animated Gobelins*. As Fokine did not require more than one scene he began rehearsals and the ballet was produced under the title of *The Animated Gobelins*.

On the raising of the proscenium curtain, the artistes were discovered grouped behind a second curtain of gauze which threw the figures into one plane so that they gave the impression of a Gobelins tapestry. In this production Fokine had no desire to effect an innovation, but simply to display the ability of his pupils. The ballet, however, was a great success, particularly a dance by several buffoons.

Immediately after the performance A. D. Krupensky came to Fokine and said : " Would it not be possible to produce this on the stage of the Imperial Theatre with real artistes ? " Now, up to this time, Fokine, as we have seen, had not been afforded an opportunity to produce something for the Imperial stage and he was naturally very pleased at the suggestion. He explained that a *scenario* would be necessary and asked that Benois should be approached to supply one. Unfortunately, although Fokine was unaware of it, Benois was then having differences with the directorate of the theatre, but he was given to understand that Benois would be invited to provide a theme. He was away at this time.

Later, Fokine received the *scenario* from Krupensky ; but, after reading it, he thought that the interest was not strong enough to be spread over three acts, and it was decided to make the production a one-act ballet containing three scenes, with the original title of *Le Pavillon d'Armide*.

* *
*

This is the theme of the ballet. The Vicomte de Beaugency, while travelling on a visit to his betrothed, is caught in a dreadful storm which forces him to break his journey and take refuge.

He finds himself in the grounds of a castle belonging to a certain Marquis, who is a magician. The Marquis receives his unexpected guest with every courtesy and places at his disposal an annex known as Armida's Pavilion.

There is something mysterious about this rich abode with its domed ceiling and lurking shadows. The eye is arrested by the space between the two tall windows looking on to the grounds, which is covered with a beautiful Gobelins tapestry representing, in the costume of Armida, an ancestress of the Marquis celebrated for her beauty. Beneath the tapestry stands a great clock supported by figures of Love and Time. The Vicomte, left to himself, cannot rest; he remains gazing at the tapestry. At last he falls asleep.

At the stroke of midnight the supporters of the clock step down from their pedestal. Love drives Time away, and one by one the Hours dance into the night.

The figures in the tapestry grow more distinct and presently come to life. The room is peopled with Armida, her court, and her captive knights. But Rinaldo is missing. The Vicomte, already in love with Armida, takes Rinaldo's place. The King, who bears a striking likeness to the Marquis, blesses their union.

Gradually the dancing and revelry cease, the light fades, and the figures vanish. The Hours return to the clock, Love is vanquished by Time, and the Gobelins tapestry is woven anew. The Vicomte is asleep.

Daylight disperses the shadows and a calm morning succeeds the night of storm. The Marquis enters to greet his guest. The Vicomte awakes and recognises him as the King of his dream. At the same time he finds the gold scarf which Armida had given him. He kisses it with passion and dashes up to the tapestry. Terror-stricken, he wishes to escape, but the enchantment is too strong and he falls dead at the feet of the Marquis.

III

Fokine then went for a short holiday and on his return met Benois for the first time. The meeting took place in the scene-painting rooms where the scenery for *Le Pavillon d'Armide* was being constructed. The story of this meeting and their collaboration is best told in Fokine's own words : "Benois charmed me with the love with which he discussed the smallest detail of the production. I had already produced several ballets but without the collaboration of a painter. Now I had a painter, a wonderful artist, who spoke with such enthusiasm of how he would clothe my dancers. We planned together the effects of the appearing grotto, and the vanishing Gobelins. At last I felt that my desire for collaboration in the theatre had begun to materialise.

"We met every day. Then we were joined by Tcherepnine. We discussed every 'number' and he decided to alter several things and add others. At first all went well, but presently I remarked that difficulties began to be placed in my way. I had few opportunities for rehearsals, and I noticed that the artistes who did not put in an appearance seemed to enjoy the good wishes of the management, while those who came and worked did not. I could not understand the reason and thought that success might be displeasing to the director and the *maître de ballet*, but it appeared that the real trouble came from higher quarters. It seemed to me strange that Krupensky should be antagonistic since it was he who had invited me to stage the ballet. Enormous expense had been incurred and the management itself was ruining the whole production. Most of the artistes were very pleasant towards me, but a few unfriendly-disposed persons are quite sufficient to spoil the whole atmosphere of work, which they did to gain favour with Krupensky. However, on the advice of Benois, I decided to complete my work in spite of the mental torture to which I was continually being subjected.

"This production was very complicated from the scenic point of view, yet we were only granted one or two rehearsals in the theatre. I had no time to explain to the artistes in what direction they must make their exit while the scenery was being changed during a 'black-out,' how the stage would open and the grotto disappear, and so forth. I remember that I was never more terrified than when I

[*Photo : Studio des Capucines, Paris*

SCENE FROM " LE PAVILLON D'ARMIDE "

[*Photo : Mishkin, New York*

MICHEL FOKINE AS AMOUN IN " CLÉOPÂTRE "

gave the signal for the changing of the scenery. It was quite dark and the music very loud. Everything went in different directions, part of the scenery was 'flied,' part was carried into the space behind the wings. The grotto was being lowered below, a huge clock was rising, and heavy furniture was being wheeled on to the stage. Some artistes, pushing and jostling, were leaving the stage, others were coming on. All this occurred in darkness and amidst open trap-doors. It struck me that a large group of people was standing on the very place where the stage was going to slide apart and that everybody must fall into an abyss which was many floors deep. I became quite cold at the thought of their danger. Then suddenly the lights were switched on, the scenery was in place, the artistes were partly behind the scenes and those who had to be on the stage were in their positions. The grotto with the group of Armida and her followers had vanished. I sighed deeply and wiped the perspiration from my brow."

It was under such conditions that the final rehearsal took place. Fokine felt the ballet to be beautiful, but not yet ready for performance on the date already announced. He went home ill at ease and sad at heart. The next morning, on opening his paper, he was surprised to see a long letter to the Editor from Benois in which he exposed the intrigues of the management and expressed the view that the ballet would be wonderful if only the rehearsals had not been so wilfully restricted. The date fixed for the performance was postponed and Fokine was allowed a few additional rehearsals. Then the ballet was given on the 25th of November, and achieved a brilliant success. A close friendship was formed between the two collaborators as a result of the cares and trials they had experienced and combated together.

They visited each other frequently and at Benois' house Fokine made the acquaintance of his artist friends, for nearly all the distinguished painters who were living in St. Petersburg at that time, or who had come there from Moscow, called on him. There he met Bakst, Dobuzhinsky, Kustudiev, Lanceray, Serov, Somov, and many

33

others who afterwards visited Fokine. At one of these artistic gatherings a friend of Fokine's, P. Mikhaylov, read a paper pointing out the necessity for ballet to leave the circle which circumscribed its development, and the important results to be gained from the collaboration of artistes of the ballet with painters. This paper was a statement of the views on ballet reform which Fokine had so often discussed with his friend, and which even then were beginning to take material form.

CHAPTER FIVE

" UNE NUIT D'EGYPTE " AND TWO VERSIONS OF " CHOPINIANA "

I

THE next year (1908) opened auspiciously, for, on March 8th, Fokine showed his extraordinary versatility as a choreographer. On the same evening of that day he produced at the Maryinsky Theatre, again in the cause of charity, two new ballets, *Une Nuit d'Egypte* and *Chopiniana*. The first was a drama without words, and demonstrated Fokine's contention that dancing, mime, costume, and style-atmosphere should be blended into one harmonious whole.

One day, when looking through the Theatre library, he found the score of *Une Nuit d'Egypte*, a ballet by A. Arensky, which seemed to him to offer considerable possibilities for the expression of his ideals. According to the directions given in the score, the scene represents the banks of the Nile, with a temple to the right. The background shows an island with pyramids and sphinx in the distance.

Berenice, followed by her companions, comes from the temple to draw water from the Nile. She encounters Amoun, her betrothed, who, having just returned from the chase, shows her his spoils. This incident gives rise to a dance which simulates a hunt. Berenice pretends to be a gazelle, while Amoun takes the part of a hunter and tries to strike at her heart. This dance is ended by Berenice's pressing her hand to her heart and falling, as if stricken, into Amoun's arms.

At this moment a messenger comes and announces the arrival of Cleopatra, who enters the temple attended by a numerous train. At the sight of the Queen, Amoun falls madly in love with her, despite his endeavours to overcome the emotion that overwhelms him. He tries to enter the temple, but his passage is barred and he gives way

35

to despair. Presently Cleopatra comes forth and reclines on the *lectus* placed in the shade of the palm-tree, while Arsinoe vainly seeks to entertain her with dances. Amoun's passion is again aroused, and Berenice becomes sad at the thought of her lover's wishing to forsake her.

Amoun climbs on the temple steps and, bending his bow, looses an arrow, which strikes the palm-tree. Cleopatra, much moved, commands him to be seized. Arsinoe gives the Queen the arrow, to which is attached a strip of papyrus on which Amoun has written: "I love you." Soldiers bring him before Cleopatra, and in reply to her reproaches he answers simply: "I love you and offer you my life in exchange for a night of love." The Queen accepts the compact, but tells Amoun that in return he must die at the first rays of dawn by drinking a cup of poison.

Berenice throws herself at Cleopatra's feet, beseeching her not to take Amoun from her, and entreats him, for the sake of the love he once bore her, to renounce his fatal passion. But he is not to be deterred and goes to the Queen.

Now distant fanfares are heard, which, approaching nearer and nearer, announce the return of Antony. Cleopatra orders the poisoned cup to be brought, but the High Priest substitutes a harmless sleeping draught prepared by himself. Amoun drinks the potion and falls into the arms of the priest. He is carried away at the moment Antony appears in his trireme. After an exchange of greetings a feast is held, with dancing as part of the entertainment. Then Cleopatra and Antony, with their attendants, embark on the ship, which sails away.

When they have departed, the High Priest orders the servants to bring in the prostrate Amoun, and now comes Berenice, who bewails the death of her lover. But the High Priest bids her be of good cheer and awakens Amoun. He falls in tears at her feet and she pardons his unfaithfulness.

Fokine made inquiries and found that this ballet had been written for Petipa, who had intended to present it in connection with a festival at Olgin Ostrov. The costumes even had been made, but for some reason the piece had never been performed. Fokine found the costumes quite new, but, while those for the men were good, he disliked those intended for the female characters, which consisted of *maillot*, ballet-shoes, and short and full ballet-skirt adorned with an Egyptian decorative motif; there were also some ornaments in the form of a snake, to be worn on the elaborate *coiffure* then fashionable.

He took close-fitting blouses, belted them with scarves, and in this simple manner achieved a reform in ballet costume. He had wigs made from twisted tow, and designed a special make-up for the artistes, in which the eyes were lengthened; even their bodies were darkened with a little brown, a proceeding which at that time was an unprecedented innovation. For scenery he borrowed one of the stock sets painted for the opera *Aïda*.

Fokine played the part of Amoun, while the other characters were allotted thus: Pavlova (*Berenice*), Gerdt (*Antony*), Bulgakov (*High Priest*), Nijinsky (*Male Slave*) Preobrajenskaya (*Female Slave*); the rôle of Cleopatra was taken by an artiste from the Dramatic School, while Karsavina danced in the *Danse des Juives*.

II

The idea of arranging a ballet to Chopin's music came to Fokine when, on turning over some pieces at a music-seller, he found a Suite entitled *Chopiniana*[1], orchestrated by Glazunov. It consisted of four pieces—a Polonaise, Nocturne, Mazurka, and Tarantella. To these, Fokine decided to add a Waltz which, at his request, Glazunov also orchestrated.

[1] There is some divergence of opinion respecting the date of the first performance of the first version of *Chopiniana*. The date as given above is based on information supplied from semi-official sources. M. Fokine, however, in a letter to the author, states: "The ballet *Chopiniana* was a series of pictures of different character, staged at the same time as the first performance of *Eunice*. . . . The second *Chopiniana* was staged for a charity at the same time as the first performance of *Une Nuit d'Egypte*. The second *Chopiniana* was given at a Pupils' Display, not the first. It was performed by artistes first, and only then by students." Our text is in agreement with this last observation.

At this first presentation of the ballet, the *Polonaise* was danced as such by a number of artistes dressed in rich Polish costumes; the scene represented a ball-room.

The theme for the *Nocturne* was suggested to Fokine by an incident in the life of Chopin. The scene showed the interior of a deserted monastery, the dreary expanse of wall broken by the sombre outlines of the tombs of dead monks. Chopin is seen seated at a piano engaged in composition. He is very ill and cannot concentrate his thoughts. Becoming assailed with vague fears, he rises from his seat and peers into the distant gloom. Now the ghosts of the dead monks come forth and torment him with menacing gestures. He recoils in terror, clings to the piano, strikes a few chords with trembling fingers and collapses, half-fainting, on the keys. Presently Chopin's Muse, represented by a dancer in white, comes from the darkness, drives away the haunting visions, and comforts him. He raises his head and resumes his place at the piano. At peace, he continues his composition.

The theme for the *Mazurka* was a Polish wedding. A young girl is to be married to an old man. While the festivities are at their height, the young girl's lover enters and begs her to go away with him. She throws away her engagement-ring and grants his prayer.

The *Waltz* was the first sketch for a new conception of *Chopiniana* (*Les Sylphides*). It was a purely classical *pas de deux* danced by Pavlova and Obukov. The *danseuse* wore a long ballet dress in the manner of Taglioni.

The *Tarantella* was an *ensemble* danced by several artistes and was given a realistic atmosphere by the presence of a number of small children. The scene represented Naples with a distant view of Vesuvius.

As usual, Fokine was forced to use costumes and scenery already in stock, but he was able to obtain the Polish costumes which had been made for *Le Miroir Fantasque*, an old ballet arranged by Petipa. *Chopiniana* was well received.

III

The performance was a triumph. The director of the theatre was so enchanted with *Une Nuit d'Egypte* that he commissioned Fokine to give this ballet the following year, and promised to provide him with new costumes and special scenery.

Fokine continued to find great pleasure in Benois' friendship, and always confided to him his plans and dreams. The latter, no less interested in his friend's ambitions, always listened with interest and gave him much valuable counsel. For example, when Fokine described to him his views on the production of *Une Nuit d'Egypte*, he advised him to mask the love scene between Cleopatra and Amoun by means of a living veil formed by causing the slaves to dance round her couch.

Again, when Fokine was asked to produce a pantomime for a *Bal Poudré*, he told Benois of his plans. The painter, who had made a special study of the history and manners of the eighteenth century, soon contrived a piquant theme which he developed while they sat in his room by the fire-side. The music chosen was Clementi's *Sonatinas*, which was arranged in accordance with their wishes by Maurice Keller.

The pantomime was produced at Fokine's residence. The furniture was moved to one side, and Benois and Bakst sat on the table while the piece was given in the middle of the room. The characters were taken by Marie Mariusovna Petipa (*Columbine*), Cecchetti (*Pantaloon*), Bekefi (*Harlequin*), and other celebrated artistes. According to Fokine, Cecchetti invested his miming with such humour that Bakst laughed so much that he fell off the table.

IV

On the 6th of April, at a Pupils' Display, Fokine presented a new version of *Chopiniana*, now transformed into a purely classical ballet, and danced in the long muslin skirts characteristic of Taglioni's epoch. It consisted of a Nocturne danced by the whole company, a Valse executed by one of the *premières danseuses*, a Mazurka danced as a *pas seul* by the *danseuse étoile*, another Mazurka *pas seul* by the *premier danseur*, a Prelude danced by one of the *premières danseuses*, a Valse *pas de deux* by the *danseuse étoile* and *premier danseur*, and a final Valse executed by the entire company. The solo numbers were linked together by a succession of plastic groups, invested with a rare poetic charm and chaste beauty, formed by the *corps de ballet*. This production was an answer to those critics who asserted that Fokine wished to destroy the traditional ballet.

This second *Chopiniana* was orchestrated by Maurice Keller, with the exception of the Valse taken from the first *Chopiniana*, which, it will be remembered, was orchestrated by Glazunov.

At the end of the season, Fokine decided to take a holiday, and went to reside in Switzerland at the little town of Montreux, situated on the borders of the Lake of Geneva. There he was visited by Ida Rubinstein, who had been taking lessons from him and did not wish them to be interrupted. Fokine arranged a Salomé dance for her, for which, at their joint request, Glazunov composed the music.

While Fokine was at Montreux he received a very interesting letter from Benois, who wrote that he had formed a plan to take *Le Pavillon d'Armide* and other of Fokine's ballets[1] to Paris, and that Diaghilev would undertake the matter. He answered that he would be very happy to show his work abroad.

On Fokine's return to St. Petersburg, Ida Rubinstein danced the Salomé dance at a special *soirée*. She was very anxious to give the whole of Oscar Wilde's play *Salomé*, but the censorship would not grant her the necessary permission. The scenery and costumes had already been designed by Bakst. Since everything was ready, it was decided to give the dance only, but with the full setting and all the characters in the play present on the stage. The entertainment was to be filled out with musical items. Fokine

---

[1] It is important to remember that before Fokine met Diaghilev he had already composed *Les Sylphides*, *Cléopâtre*, and *Le Pavillon d'Armide*.

grouped the players, but, as he was about to give the signal for the curtain to be raised, Rubinstein told him that the fruit on the table must be removed, as the censor found that this gave a suggestion of a feast resulting in the dance of Salomé, whereas permission had been granted solely for the performance of the *Dance of the Seven Veils*. Fokine took away the fruit, and the dance was given with Herod, Herodias, and the other characters still on the stage.

Soon afterwards, Fokine met Diaghilev and had a long conversation with him regarding the ballets to be shown at Paris. Diaghilev did not like *Une Nuit d'Egypte*, for he considered the music mediocre. It was therefore decided to take only *Chopiniana* and *Le Pavillon d'Armide*, but Diaghilev wished Fokine to arrange a series of dances to an excerpt from the music to the second act of Borodin's opera *Prince Igor*. He consented and Diaghilev took a small theatre situated near the Ekaterininsky Canal so that the rehearsals could be commenced.

At first Fokine was very nervous and afraid to begin on the dances. Many of his friends came to the rehearsals, such as the artists Bakst, Roehrich, Serov, and Somov, and the old *balletomane* Besobrasov. A few days later Fokine met Roehrich at the offices of the Apollo magazine, who told him that he had been commissioned by Diaghilev to design the costumes and scenery, and how delighted he was at the prospect of collaborating with Fokine. Roehrich said to Fokine: " From what I saw at the rehearsal I can see that you will do something wonderful with the new ballet."

On the other hand, Besobrasov, after watching some rehearsals, went up to him and said : " Will you permit an old man to express an opinion ? I think you are doing your *Igor* wrongly, Mikhayl Mikhaylovich." Fokine replied : " I do not feel that it is wrong, but we shall see when it is finished." The next day Benois came and pulled a very long face, and expressed his doubts as to the ballet's success. But when the ballet was completed both congratulated him heartily. He had a fine company of sixty dancers to work with, including Adolph Bolm and Sophie Fedorova, who were cast respectively for the parts of the Chief and the Polovtsian Girl.

It is interesting to note that the steps and movements used in this dance were suggested to Fokine partly from what he had read of the Asiatic tribes which invaded Russia, and still more by Borodine's music; for at this time he had not studied Caucasian, Persian, and Turkish dances, as he did later.

Diaghilev left for Paris to make arrangements for the proposed season, and on his return had a further conversation with Fokine, in the course of which he agreed to take *Une Nuit d'Egypte*, provided the title were altered to *Cléopâtre* and subject to various alterations in the music.

These were as follows. First, for the arrival of Cleopatra and the dancing by the female slaves, the music written by Rimsky-Korsakov for the appearance of Cleopatra in his opera *Mlada* was substituted. Second, for the veil dance of the two slaves, Glinka's *Danse Orientale*, from his opera *Ruslan and Lyudmila*, was taken. Third, for the final dance, the *Danse Persane* from Mussorgsky's *Khovantchina* was used. In each case the music was matched with the rhythm, character, and length of Arensky's original numbers; the choreography remained almost unaltered.

Finally, two novelties were introduced: a Bacchante dance arranged to the *Bacchanale* from Glazunov's *Les Saisons*, and Fokine took advantage of the fact that Arensky's music often varies in *tempo* to devise a new and tragic ending for the ballet, so that Amoun was poisoned instead of being drugged. Fokine asked Tcherepnine to write new music for this episode, taking as a basis the themes of Arensky and other composers. He mimed the scene for Tcherepnine and divided it into several dramatic moments, for each of which the composer devised appropriate music. This affords an interesting example not of pantomime arranged to music, but of music composed to a theme expressed in pantomime.

The version of this ballet prepared for Paris differed in two other respects, in that the appearance of Antony was omitted, while Berenice was renamed Ta-Hor.

[*Photo : Studio des Capucines, Paris*

SCENE FROM " LES SYLPHIDES "

SCENE FROM " LE CARNAVAL "   [*Photo : Barba, Monte Carlo*

(*As presented by Les Ballets Russes du Col. de Basil*)

CHAPTER SIX

FIRST PERFORMANCE OF FOKINE BALLETS IN WESTERN
EUROPE

I

THE company organised by Diaghilev for his combined
Paris season of opera and ballet arrived at that capital
early in May, 1909.   The ballet repertory was composed
of *Le Pavillon d'Armide*, *Les Sylphides*,[1] *Cléopâtre*, *Polovtsian
Dances* from *Prince Igor*, and *Le Festin*, a suite of *divertissements*.

The Chatelet Theatre which Diaghilev had selected as
his base was a theatre beloved of the middle-class public.
It had just closed down after the successful run of a melodrama entitled *Les Aventures de Gavroche*, of which 128
performances had been given.

The impresario found the interior in a deplorable state
of repair, but a few days later it was almost unrecognisable
owing to the efforts of an army of work-people of all kinds.
The stage was refloored and carried over the space
previously occupied by the orchestra, which necessitated
the abolition of nine rows of stalls ; the gloomy corridors
were hung with tapestries ; and a profusion of new electric
light fittings made the theatre appear warm and cheerful
in contrast with its former state.

Svetlov, in his *Le Ballet Contemporain*, has presented so
vivid a picture of the strenuous days of rehearsal prior to
the first performance that we reproduce his words :

" Formidable cases of properties, costumes, tights, and
scenery—forty thousand kilogrammes in weight—were
being unpacked in the basement.   On the stage behind
the back-cloth nibbled the sheep which appear in the last
act of *Armide*.   Tcherepnine conducted the orchestral
rehearsals of *Armide*.   Fokine was indefatigable, the

---

[1] *Chopiniana* was re-named *Les Sylphides*, a title suggested by the
first romantic ballet, *La Sylphide*, inseparably linked with Marie
Taglioni.

43

artistes no less so. The work, with brief interruptions, went on from morning to midnight. Everyone, being tired out, became nervous as before a decisive combat, but the work progressed in an atmosphere of friendliness and harmony. Sometimes there were little incidents, the conductor would not concede a point to the choreographer and *vice versa*. But all was settled amicably and at once. Everyone recognised the importance of the common work and the necessity of working freely and artistically.

" A buffet was improvised behind the stage on an upturned case. It was impossible to go and lunch at an hotel, and the artistes went there for refreshment during their rest intervals.

" Behind the wings appeared the imposing figure of Chaliapine and the slender silhouette of Fokine. Nearby the elegant Karsavina practised her exercises."

The musical critic, M. D. Calvocoressi, who acted as assistant to Diaghilev for this first season, has recorded in his Recollections an interesting impression of Fokine at this period. " Then there was Fokine, the ballet master. It was especially he who aroused my enthusiasm. . . . Amazingly lithe and springy, cheerful and patient even when he might have had the best reason for losing his temper, he danced and rushed all round the stage, watching and stimulating every one of his dancers. He seemed to have a hundred eyes in his head. At an incredible speed he would go round each line or group in turn, showing one dancer how to perform a step, correcting another one's attitude, helping a third to understand the rhythm and phrasing of the music. He had an unerring sense of construction as well as of colour and motion. I doubt whether, without him, Diaghilev's ballet could have come into being."[1]

II

The press announced that a dress rehearsal would take place on the nineteenth of the month. This function, in Paris more important than a first performance, attained to

[1] *Musicians' Gallery*, 1933.

the dignity of a gala performance. There were present the most distinguished members of the aristocracy; eminent artists, critics, and writers; great singers like Jean de Rezke, Geraldine Farrar, Lucienne Breval, and Lina Cavalieri; famous dancers like Zambelli, Mariquita, Truhanova, Duncan, and Rosita Mauri—but this is sufficient to indicate the quality of the audience. The programme consisted of *Le Pavillon d'Armide*, *Prince Igor*, and *Le Festin*. Benois' lovely scenery and costumes evoked the sumptuous epoch of Louis XIV, such a subject had stirred his imagination to evolve the most charming and ingenious scenes, the loveliest costumes.

Of Fokine's groups and dances, Svetlov, an eye-witness and excellent critic, declared that they displayed a remarkable artistic taste. " He knows how to contrive beautiful pictures and possesses an apt sense for choregraphic colour. Innovations abound in the complex groups born of his imagination. The groups are incomparable from the point of view of composition. The *danses generales* offer an original beauty, the separate *variations* have novelty, that of Nijinsky is entirely new; the choregrapher has known how to avoid the banality of the *pirouettes* and *entrechats* of which the *variations* for male dancers are usually composed. The dance of the genii and that of the buffoons (a masterpiece of stage production) and the final waltz (*Valse Noble*) are admirable in composition and colour."[1]

Another famous critic, Robert Brussel, wrote that " the groups, figures and steps of the choregrapher M. Fokine reveal a rich and versatile imagination and, what is still more rare, a very informed artistic taste. There is a most attractive combination of tradition and modernism in his composition. As for success, it was enormous and recalled the most wonderful evenings of *Boris*."

Certain critics and *balletomanes* made two criticisms of Fokine's choregraphy in *Armide*; first, that the *première danseuse*, being reduced to the same level as the rest of the company, had no predominant part; second, that the ballet did not contain a single academic *ensemble*. But, as Svetlov

[1] *Le Ballet Contemporain*, 1912.

points out, these criticisms were quite unjustified. " The *première danseuse* has a great many dances, only she executes them against a background of dancing groups formed by the other artistes, as if in the square of a *ballabile*."[1] With regard to the second charge, he protested that " although an academic *ensemble* was formerly considered an indispensable attribute of ballet, if it were not present in *Armide*, it was simply because the exigencies of the theme made it unnecessary."[2]

But, much as the Parisian public admired *Le Pavillon d'Armide*, it was the *Polovtsian Dances* from *Prince Igor* that aroused their unbounded admiration. The spectators were carried away by the wild throbbing frenzy of Borodine's music, that maddening passion contrasted with periods of deep lassitude so charactertistic of the Slav temperament. Fokine has exactly interpreted in his choregraphic medium that marvellous evocation of 12th century Russia, even to the least modification of its themes and rhythms. The music and dances seem inseparable, it is impossible to believe that they ever existed apart.

*
* *

The scene represents a Polovtsian camp at dawn. On a rising plain is a semi-circular group of rude, dome-shaped tents made from the hides of animals, tanned and dyed to varying shades of red and brown. On the slope of the eminence are further tents which spring up like giant mole-hills. In the distance, half-obscured by a damp haze and the smoke from the dying camp-fires, stretches a dreary range of violet hills, their bases lapped by a broad river. The whole scene is bathed in the fitful glare of glowing embers.

Grouped about the tent-flaps are maidens and women of the tribe, while on the ground sprawl the still slumbering warriors. Now they rise from their hard couches to bend and stretch their aching limbs, and greet one another with rough shoulder-clap and uncouth jest. Ferocious of aspect, their faces smeared with soot and mud, their coats

[1] *Op. cit.*
[2] *Op. cit.*

green and mottled red and ochre, their trousers striped in bright hues, one is reminded of a lair of wild beasts rather than a camp of human beings.

A mournful chant fills the air and several women wend their way forward in single file. They dance with slow languorous movements, their bodies swaying rhythmically to the fluttering of the rose-coloured veils which they hold above their heads between outstretched hands. They turn round and fall on one knee. Another group of women dance forward in the same manner. Now they sway their bodies from side to side with rippling movements of their arms. They incline their heads backward and forward, then rise to their feet. They renew their graceful dance and gradually merge into two circles between which comes a newcomer, a woman clad in scarlet with her hair dressed in two dark plaits threaded with a string of pearls. She glides softly to and fro, now advancing, now retreating, her body swaying with a soft rounded grace, her arms extended in an undulating line.

At the conclusion of the dance the women melt into one quivering mass, above which the veils wave and writhe like wind-blown points of flame, and retire to the shelter of their tents. There they sink to the ground and raise themselves on one elbow, each face half-concealed with a veil-draped arm.

Swiftly the wailing chant gives place to a fierce, throbbing rhythm. A flash of scarlet and there vaults into the centre of the clearing a dazzling figure in striped costume of red and ochre. It is the chief. His whole being pulsates with a burning excess of savage exultation in his strength. He continually whirls round, springs upward, spins in the air and crashes to the ground. His brows are contorted, his head flung back, his mouth opened wide in a hoarse, gasping shout of triumph.

Fired by his example, his lieutenants dart to his side. They maintain one line and step quickly to right and left, now as if in pursuit of a foe, now as if in retreat, the while they bend their bows and twang the strings in simulated loosing of an arrow. Now they dash forward in two lines.

Those in front drop swiftly to the ground while those behind spring over their recumbent figures. Suddenly they rise in a splendid posture of defiance. Some are kneeling, some standing, but each bow is bent with the string drawn taut to the ear. One is reminded of some classic heroic frieze. They rise, divide into little groups, and exchange congratulations on their prowess.

Again the women glide forward to inflame the heated warriors with the voluptuous swaying of their bodies and the seductive manipulation of their veils. They merge into two lines between which dances the chief's favourite. The avenue dissolves into a circle and the women fall on their knees, their heads thrown backward, their arms extended in a gesture of abandon. Their passions awakened by this spectacle, the warriors bound in and out of their midst, stamping their feet and shaking their bows aloft with incredible ferocity.

Now the warriors collect into two bands disposed at the left and right-hand corners of the encampment, while the women rise to their feet, form into a serried mass, and slowly retreat.

Again the music reverberates in impetuous, fiery rhythm. One group of warriors surges forward in a diagonal line from right to left. A moment later their path is crossed by the remaining band who pass in a diagonal line from left to right. Now the warriors turn about and with cat-like step and sinister crouching attitude surround the women, a quick movement—and they fling them on their shoulders with a facility born of long practice. They lower the women to the ground and withdraw to the tents.

The music changes to a swift theme played *pizzicato*, and four youths spring forward. They emphasise the measure with loud slaps of their hands on their muscular thighs. Now each pair links arms and whirls round and round. They separate, bound high in the air, and fall flat on their stomachs.

The maidens come forward in serried line, their arms outstretched, their bodies quivering with the frenzied shuffling of their feet. Suddenly they fall to the ground

48

on one knee, each with an arm flung aloft to curve grace-fully over the head.

The young men spring to their feet to bound into the air with wild grimaces and rhythmic claps of their hands. The maidens repeat their former dance. Then they spin to right and left, their garments fluttering, their dark plaits swinging with the velocity of their movements. Again they fall to the ground on one knee, with bodies arched and one arm held above their heads.

Two of the youths leap into the air with a convulsive bound and loud claps of their hands. Exactly as they descend, their companions repeat their movements. The women pass to each side of the encampment and the chief dashes into their midst. He leaps forward, spins in the air, and crashes to the ground. The other warriors, their primitive passions stirred by this war-like display, hurl themselves into the dance—feet thudding to the maddening, pulsating rhythm of the music, bows flourished aloft. They flow into two lines, cross and recross, every step affording occasion for a frenzied leap. Now they wind about their chief in a circle which alternately narrows and widens. They inflame their flagging spirits with hoarse cries and goad their tired muscles with frenzied lashing of the ground with their bows. The movement becomes a seething tumult of brutal rage, ever faster, ever more violent, until the dancers, breathless, soaked in sweat, and staggering from exhaustion, cease from sheer physical inability to continue. The women dash forward in four long lines, spin on one foot alternately to right and left, whirl in three successive turns, and retreat to the shelter of the tents. The chief and his lieutenants dash forward with mighty bounds, heads thrown back, bows shaken on high, mouths opened wide in a shout of triumph.

No one who has seen this dance will deny its right to be acclaimed a masterpiece. Nothing could be more removed from the traditions of the old ballet and nothing could be more indicative of Fokine's genius as a choregrapher; and

let it be remembered that this number was composed a
score and more years ago. Yet this ballet is still as fresh
and as inspiring as if it had been composed but yesterday.

After its first performance it was greeted with a veritable
tempest of spontaneous applause which seemed never-
ending. There was no less than six curtain calls.

III

On the 29th May the press recorded the arrival of Anna
Pavlova, who was to make her *début* in *Les Sylphides*, and
hinted darkly at the mystery surrounding the interpreter
of Cleopatra in the ballet of the same name, which it was
stated would be taken by a great Parisian lady.

The dress rehearsal of *Les Sylphides* and *Cléopâtre* took place
on the 2nd of June. The house was full, so full that there
were spectators seated in the gangways. There was a buzz
of suppressed excitement, an atmosphere of eager expectancy.
A brief overture and the curtain rose on *Les Sylphides*.

**
*

The scenery by Alexandre Benois depicts a sylvan glade ;
on one side rises the grey ruins of a church, on the other
a little group of trees, while in the centre background the
outline of a tomb emerges faintly. The scene is very dark,
except where the moon lets fall a quivering patch of light
here and there. The general colour is a glowing dark green.

At the back, grouped in a semi-circle, are the *corps de
ballet*, a shimmering mass of white, while in the centre are
grouped Pavlova, Karsavina, Baldina, and Nijinsky.

The dancers are dressed in the traditional ballet skirt of
the period of Taglioni, the edge of the skirt reaching mid-
way between ankle and knee, while their hair is adorned
with a little fillet of white flowers. Silvery wings are
attached to their waists. The effect of these floating white
clouds against the cold atmosphere of the scene reminds
one of snowflakes whirled hither and thither by the wind in
the moonlight of a winter's eve. At other times they
resemble clouds of mist, the surf on a breaking wave, and
perhaps best of all a little band of winter fairies at play

beneath the waning moon in the shadow of a frosted glade.

All the dances breathe an intense sadness, save only the last which is full of rapture, a joy of quick movement ; and just as the spectator feels he must join in to free himself from the intense strain on his emotions, the curtain falls. Then, so torn is he between the conflicting emotions of sadness and rapture, that a few moments elapse before he can applaud.

The fairies, the glade, the moonlight—all have faded away, but an unforgettable memory remains, and a regret that the vision has passed, and so quickly.

Both ballets had an excellent reception. *Les Sylphides* was described by one critic as " a series of dances executed in a landscape by young girls wearing Taglioni dresses, and by a dreamy youth, a poet if you will, who seems to savour, in the midst of this diaphanous enchantment, the refined delights of an ' artificial paradise.' You cannot conceive anything more ethereal, more seraphic, and more voluptuous than the evolution of all those fragile forms, of all those ' happy shades ' in the emerald-green reflections of the moonlight. . . . It is difficult to think of Chopin's music in connection with a ballet, but in this particular case, which suggests a dream, an hallucination, the choice is defensible and almost legitimate."[1]

In *Cléopâtre* the *Bacchanale* was much applauded, while Pavlova was highly praised for her moving portrait of Ta Hor. The mysterious interpreter of the title-role proved to be Ida Rubinstein, who made Cleopatra a striking figure, at once repellent and attractive by her suggestion of cruelty and her fascinating beauty.

[1] *Le Journal*, June 2nd, 1909.

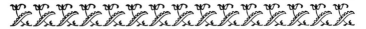

CHAPTER SEVEN

PRODUCTION OF "LE CARNAVAL," "SCHÉHÉRAZADE,"
AND "L'OISEAU DE FEU."

I

AFTER the triumphant return of the company to St.
Petersburg from the immensely successful first Paris
season, Diaghilev began to make plans for a series of
performances to be given the following year. He was of
the opinion that it was very important to produce a ballet
with a theme based on some Russian folk tale. Diaghilev,
Bakst, Benois, and Fokine had many discussions on this
subject, without, however, being able to arrive at any
decision. Then Fokine began to read all the *Skazki* he
could find. He was unable, however, to find any *one*
suitable for a ballet, so he contrived a *scenario* from several,
mainly from *The Tale of Ivan Tsarevich, The Bird of Light
and the Grey Wolf,* and the legend of the enchanter Köstchei
and his soul hidden in an egg. His suggestion was approved;
then arose the question of what music should be used.

There were further discussions and finally Lyadov, who
had written many compositions on folk themes, was chosen.
The *scenario* was offered to him and accepted. Fokine began
working on the general scheme of the dances, but week
after week passed by and not a bar of music had been
received from Lyadov. A little later, he heard quite by
chance that the composer had just purchased some music
manuscript paper. It was obvious that nothing had been
done. Upon this information Diaghilev went to see
Lyadov and pressed him for the music, pointing out the
urgent need for it and requesting a definite date for its
delivery. The composer explained that he was very
interested in the work and that it required a great deal of
thought, and, since he did not work quickly, he could only
promise that he would send it as soon as it was completed.
Diaghilev, being dissatisfied with this answer, then took
back the *scenario.*

Another consultation was hurriedly arranged at which Diaghilev told Benois and Fokine that he had in mind a young composer called Igor Stravinsky, who might be suitable. At this time Stravinsky's *Feux d'Artifice* was to be played at a concert and Diaghilev took the two friends to hear this composition. The audience was not greatly appreciative, but Benois and Fokine thought his work very modern, very brilliant, and well suited to a ballet.

Stravinsky was written to and accepted the commission to compose the music for *L'Oiseau de Feu*, as it was decided to call the ballet. He then came to see Fokine, who explained to him the theme and the atmosphere he required. The composer set to work and soon afterwards returned with sketches for the melodies. Fokine liked the theme for the entry of Ivan Tsarevich and explained to him that Ivan made his entry over a wall and then performed a scene in mime, and hence he would like the theme broken by snatches of music suggestive of a fantastic and bewitched grove.

In similar manner he explained the incidents of the shaking of the golden apple-tree, the entrance of Köstchei and his followers, the scene where Ivan Tsarevich seeks the egg containing the enchanter's soul, the death of Köstchei, and so forth. He expressed his ideas in pantomime, then Stravinsky devised appropriate themes, and the two collaborators discussed them in detail from the choreographic and musical view-points.

The dances for the Bird of Fire were likewise the result of this close collaboration. The Bird of Fire gives each group of demons a theme to which she forces them to dance again and again, then she gives another group a different theme and so forth. Stravinsky was greatly pleased with this plan which is accurately expressed in his music. It was not long before the composer finished the score of the ballet, which was then put into rehearsal.

II

Diaghilev also asked Fokine to arrange a ballet to Rimsky-Korsakov's symphonic poem *Schéhérazade*. Again arose the question of a theme, which was solved by Bakst, who suggested the first story in *The Thousand and One Nights*. Fokine was delighted with this idea and began to sketch it out in relation to the music. The complete symphony was found to· be too long, hence it was decided to use Part I as an overture, and Parts II and IV for the ballet. There was a little uncertainty as to the most effective method of killing the erring wives and their paramours. Bakst thought they might be tied up in sacks and thrown into an imaginary river ; but in the end it was decided to slay them with cold steel. At this period Fokine had not seen any Oriental dances, so he decided to seek inspiration by studying Persian miniatures, and to use expressive pantomime in place of gesticulation.

III

At this time two youthful representatives of the *Satyricon Magazine*, MM. Patiomkin and Kornfeld, called on Fokine and begged his aid in connection with a charity entertainment they were organising at the *Zal Pavlovoi* (Pavlova Hall), a big hall at St. Petersburg. They asked him if he could possibly arrange a small ballet for them as the artistes of the Imperial Theatre had promised their support. They told him that they had already arranged to hold a Carnival every evening. This gave Fokine an inspiration. He knew Schumann's *Carnaval* well and had often thought of its possibilities as a basis for a ballet ; he told his visitors that he would arrange a Carnival ballet for them and that he would try to persuade Bakst to design the costumes.

At the next meeting with Kornfeld he explained the music he proposed to use, and after some discussion as to a likely theme they decided to read a life of Schumann, in the hope that it might afford some indication for one. Kornfeld found a German biography which he translated to Fokine, who did not read that language.

The theme of the music of *Carnaval* is a phrase consisting of the four notes A, E flat, C, and B—called in German A, S, C, H, which make up the word Asch, the name of the village in Bohemia where Schumann's friend Ernestine von Fricken lived. The members of the Davidsbund

54

jostle the well-known figures Harlequin, Columbine, Pantaloon, and Pierrot. Florestan and Eusebius represent two sides of the composer ; the first, the turbulent and impulsive side of his nature ; the second, his gentle, thoughtful and sensitive qualities. There are also four portrait studies, Chiarina, Chopin, Pagannini, and Estrella. Chiarina is a portrait of Madame Schumann (Clara Wieck) at the age of fifteen, Estrella represents Ernestine. Three of the most delightful numbers, *Reconnaisance*, *Aveu*, and *Promenade* are probably the evocation of some tender episode. The finale is the *Marche des Davidsbündler contre les Philistins* in which the latter, after being taunted and ridiculed, are ignominiously put to rout. From these indications Fokine drew all the materials for his celebrated romantic episode.

A few days later Bakst brought the most charming designs for the costumes, all in the style of Biedermeier. There was no time to be lost and the stage at one end of the hall was small. The parts were soon cast : Leontiev (*Harlequin*), Cecchetti (*Pantalon*), Nijinska (*Papillon*), Fokina (*Chiarina*), Schollar (*Estrella*), Karsavina (*Columbine*), Meyerhold (*Pierrot*), and I. Kshesinsky (*Florestan*). Fokine began to compose but under difficulties, because the hall was filled with willing helpers mounted on ladders, and busily engaged in decorating the walls with coloured festoons. There were continuous cries of : " Pass me a red one, pass me a blue one." Nevertheless in three rehearsals this masterpiece was finished.

The conclusion was a little different from that we know so well, in that, during the *Marche des Davidsbündler contre les Philistins*, the artistes left the stage and executed their dances among the audience. At the final *Galop* they all ran back to the stage, while Pierrot and Pantaloon only returned during the fall of the curtain, in front of which they remained.

The scene represented a little garden which in the later productions was changed to a curtain, sometimes blue, sometimes green, with a broad dado, relieved by two preposterous, striped settees.

IV

On the 26th March, 1910, Fokine produced for the annual Pupils' Display a ballet in the academic style to Tchaikovsky's *Les Quatre Saisons*. It was in four scenes :

WINTER.—*Snowflakes*. The *corps de ballet* danced holding long scarves of muslin decorated with little puffs of swansdown. This dance suggested falling snowflakes and ended in a group.

SPRING.—*Snowdrops*. The group broke up and disappeared, when there was a *pas de deux*. The *danseuse* represented a snowdrop struggling to raise its head while the *danseur* symbolised the snow melting at her feet.

SUMMER.—*Waltz of the flowers*.

AUTUMN.—The *corps de ballet* danced in a manner to suggest falling leaves.

This ballet was well received, especially the last scene, which evoked great applause.

V

The company arrived in Paris on the 31st May and immediately began rehearsals. The first performance was given on the 4th of June, the programme consisting of *Le Carnaval*, *Schéhérazade*, *Le Festin*, and the *Polovtsian Dances* from *Prince Igor*. The theatre selected for the season was the Opéra. The interpreters of *Le Carnaval* were as follows : L. Lopukhova (*Columbine*), V. Fokina (*Chiarina*), M. Piltz (*Estrella*), B. Nijinska (*Papillon*), Bulgakov (*Pierrot*), Fokine (*Arlequin*), Orlov (*Pantalon*), Scherer (*Eusebius*), and Vasiliev (*Florestan*).

*
* *

What a charming ballet this is ! As the curtain rises to the lively *Préambule*, three ladies flit across the scene in quick succession, each hotly pursued by an enraptured swain. They are followed by other couples swaying delightfully to the rhythm of the waltz. Enter Chiarina, then Estrella, each followed by an infatuated admirer. Vanishing, they are replaced by two lovers walking arm-in-arm. A stolen kiss and they, too, whirl away to the mysterious realms beyond.

Suddenly the curtain parts to reveal the head of a Pierrot. Peering anxiously from side to side, as if fearful of being seen, he steps forth with grotesque strides. Flapping his long sleeves with a dismal air, he wanders aimlessly to and fro, opening and shutting his mouth as if hungering for someone to kiss, while the music, now slow, halting, and melancholy, renders his thoughts aloud. Then, as it changes to joyful melody, Harlequin bounds before us. Gaily he capers about the woebegone Pierrot, now mocking him with pointed finger, now dragging him by his sleeves, until, angered by his stupidity, Harlequin flicks him smartly with his hand, disappearing with another agile leap as Pierrot, losing his balance, falls clumsily to the ground.

Again the scene is occupied by six couples dancing merrily. As they pass from sight, Pierrot drags himself away with shambling gait and listless air. Now through the curtain glides the romantic Eusebius who, sitting on a sofa, muses on his mistress until his vision takes shape in the form of the lady herself, who presents him with a rose. In a whirlwind of silk and lace comes Estrella followed by the ardent Florestan. He falls on his knees and avows his love, but the mischievous coquette raises her hands in feigned horror at this unseemly proceeding. Then, relenting, she slips an arm into his and away trip the happy pair. Now follows a *pas de deux* between Eusebius and Chiarina who dances on tip-toe while her lover follows her every movement with rapt adoration.

Enter Papillon, a vivacious lady all high spirits and fluttering ribbons, tip-toeing and pirouetting in a maze of varied movement, closely watched by Pierrot, now wearing his tall, conical hat. Half-concealed behind a sofa he becomes transported with the excitement of the chase. Emerging from his hiding-place, he launches in clumsy pursuit, but his hapless efforts are met with mocking raillery. Then, certain of his quarry, he flings down his hat, but, as swiftly as it falls, so the lady flits away. Pierrot, elated by his skill, hugs his breast in triumph, but on opening the cap finds it empty.

Now come three masked ladies, Chiarina and her two

friends, who waltz merrily to and fro when there appears
Florestan in quest of Estrella.   They bar his way, but he
slips under their arms and takes his departure.   As the
music changes to a slow, pathetic movement—*Chopin*—
Chiarina tip-toes to the centre of the curtain, while the
friends each move to her right and left.   With raised finger
Chiarina beckons to one who receives a charming embrace.
The other lady advances and the two turn slowly round
her, separating again as they sadly pass from view.

The melody changes to the lively *Reconnaisance*, and with
quaint steps there enters Columbine attended by the
sprightly Harlequin.   Evidently he is in her good graces,
for as they bow to each other she bestows on him a kiss.
With beckoning finger he beseeches her to elope with him,
but laughingly she refuses.   Brisk, important footsteps
announce the arrival of Pantaloon, a pompous little man,
who, twirling his carefully-waxed moustache, withdraws
from his pocket a folded note which he peruses with great
care and then consults his watch.   He seats himself on a
sofa and re-reads the note.   While he is thus occupied
Columbine leaps on the sofa and places her hands over
his eyes.   Chuckling with delight, Pantaloon strives to free
himself from these pleasant bonds, while Harlequin,
creeping to his side, snatches the note from his hand.
Struggling to his feet, Pantaloon loses no time in paying
attentions to his visitor, but the fickle lady is no easy
victim ; she repulses him with playful smacks on the
cheek.   Then with a graceful curtsey she introduces him
to Harlequin.   Pantaloon raising his hat extends his hand,
whereupon Harlequin displays to his astonished gaze the
compromising missive.   Crestfallen, he claps on his hat
and retires in high dudgeon, while Harlequin leaps in the
air and tears the note to pieces.

Now Columbine, tripping after Pantaloon, detains him
with outstretched hand and soothes his feelings with a
kiss.   Harlequin bounds to her side and the three perform
a *pas de trois*, from which Pantaloon is dismissed with a
push.   Harlequin performs a *pas seul* and sits on the
ground.   Columbine comes to his side when he makes

as if to take out his heart and lay it at her feet. Columbine retires to a sofa and Harlequin sits on the ground beside her, lost in contemplation of her beauty.

Again the room is filled with revellers, who hasten to offer their felicitations to the newly-betrothed pair. Pantaloon is charmingly pardoned, Pierrot may kiss her hand, and the auspicious event is celebrated in a joyful dance, interrupted all too soon by some decidedly proper-looking dames and their consorts. But even the spoil-sports, despite their protestations, are bandied to and fro in the whirl of the dance, while Harlequin, unable to refrain from further mischief, contrives with the assistance of his partner to throw into collision Pierrot and Pantaloon. Before they can recover from their surprise, he deftly flings the former's sleeves around the latter, and, fastening the ends, succeeds in binding together the ill-assorted pair. As they vainly struggle to extricate themselves, the entire company group themselves about Harlequin and Columbine in an admiring circle, in which *tableau* Pierrot and Pantaloon reluctantly take their places.

* *
*

Le Carnaval, like *Les Sylphides*, is another of Fokine's studies in romanticism, but, while the latter is a lyrical expression of sad dreams, *Carnaval* is a festival of joy, an evocation of pretty sentiment, light intrigue, and high spirits seen in a Victorian mirror. It was received with enthusiasm. One critic wrote : " It was a bold, ingenious and charming idea to make use of *Carnaval* as material for choreographic interpretation . . . the spectacle is charming and full of delicious touches."[1]

VI

The other new ballet, *Schéhérazade*, offered a marked contrast. This, as already stated, has its source in the first tale in the book of *The Thousand and One Nights*. Steeped in the traditions of Eastern fable, it offers a whole gamut of sensations, for amidst the magnificent setting of Shahryar's

[1] *Le Figaro*, June 6th, 1910.

harem, dazzling as a heap of jewels, there pass and repass in the persons of majestic shahs, kohl-eyed houris, servile eunuchs, and fierce warriors, the symbols of the seven deadly sins. The overture at once creates an Eastern atmosphere—mysterious, voluptuous, and misty with the perfumed wreaths of burning incense—while underlaying the wistful cadence of the dance, the joyous call of the hunting horns, and the frenzied sense of unbridled passion, booms the ever-insistent, ever-menacing, warning note of impending tragedy.

The Parisian public were spellbound by the scene presented to their gaze on the raising of the curtain. From the ceiling depends a voluminous emerald-green curtain caught up in heavy folds to bare this casket of living treasure. In the centre, set a little way back and at a slight angle is a smaller apartment, pierced by three blue doors. To the right are tall, orange columns, serving to support the ceiling of blue and gold. To the left, set on a dais provided with a short flight of steps, is a sumptuous divan piled high with vari-coloured cushions. It is against this background that Fokine set his ever-changing colour harmonies, his beautiful groups, and his dances which captivate, thrill, and terrify in turn.

When the curtain rises the Shah Shahryar is seated on the divan with his favourite wife Zobeida[1] on his left hand, and his brother, the Shah Zeman, on his right. Zobeida solicits the caresses of her lord, but he is in an angry mood, for his brother has hinted that his wives are unfaithful.

Shahryar summons the Chief Eunuch, who commands three *odalisques* to entertain their lord with dances. But he soon tires of them and announces his intention of starting on a hunting expedition. The women entreat him to stay, but Zobeida suspects that the journey is a pretext of the Shah's to seek the favours of another. But he is not to be deterred, and, accompanied by his brother, passes out of the harem.

---

[1] Interpreted by Ida Rubinstein.

As soon as he is gone the women throng about the blue doors, then bring out caskets of jewels, with which they adorn themselves. Presently two of their number depart and return with the Chief Eunuch, whom they bribe to open the doors. From the first comes a group of negroes in rose, from the second a similar group attired in green. With ingratiating leers they soon make love to the women, and, seizing the objects of their admiration, disappear among the shadows.

The Chief Eunuch is now approached by Zobeida, who bids him open the last door, which he does in great fear of the consequences. From this door emerges a single negro clad in gold, who fawns at Zobeida's feet. Now adolescents bring in fruit and wine, and *almées* enter to inspire passion with the thrumming of their tambourines. The women and slaves begin a dance which grows more and more passionate, and soon becomes a wild orgy.

This dance affords a wonderful illustration of Fokine's power of handling mass effects. As Zobeida succumbs to the fascinations of the gold-clad negro,[1] he bounds into the turmoil of motion, whereupon the dancers form into two long lines, and, to the rhythmic clapping of their hands, makes his way down the human avenue, now springing into the air to fall on one knee, now spinning like a teetotum, to plunge a second later into another frenzied movement. The dancers, growing wilder and wilder in their actions, with raised arms undulating like serpents, close round him so that he becomes the centre of this living wheel, the hub about which they revolve, swifter and swifter, circle within circle, until the eye is almost blinded with the glittering vortex of colour and movement.

As the orgy reaches its height, there return four Eunuchs, amazed at the sight that greets their eyes. Quick at their heels appear Shahryar, mad with rage, and his brother. With a dramatic gesture Shahryar raises his hand and guards armed with flashing scimitars pour into the harem and cut down the negroes and women. The gold-clad negro is the last to be slain. Shahryar confronts Zobeida,

---

[1] Interpreted by Vaslav Nijinsky.

sad at heart that she, too, has proved unfaithful. He is minded to pardon her, when his brother indicates the body of her lover. At this, his rage rekindles and he motions to the guards, but Zobeida snatches a poignard from the nearest and kills herself. As she expires Shahryar buries his face in his hands.

* * *

Schéhérazade was acclaimed a marvellous spectacle. " M. Fokine," wrote R. Brussel, " has put into it the best of an unquestioned talent. The same acclamations which last year greeted the bacchanale in *Cléopâtre* saluted this year the orgy *Schéhérazade*, and in these harmonious crossings of lines, in these expressive groups, in these poses and gestures each of which has its proper significance in this tumult and lull, in these exasperated violences and expressive silences, it is difficult to distinguish the talents of so many interpreters."[1]

Here are two other criticisms : " Go and see the amorous orgy of the negroes and the sultan's wives, see the voluptuousness of the dances, the passionate frenzy of the gestures, attitudes, and intertwinings ; compare these with the various scenes of orgy in our ballets ; you will soon realise on which side lies the superiority."

" *Schéhérazade* is undoubtedly one of the most beautiful spectacles, perhaps the most beautiful, which the Russians have offered us."

There were, however, severe strictures passed regarding the use of Rimsky-Korsakov's symphony to illustrate certain incidents in the ballet which differed considerably from the design the composer had in mind when writing the music. These objections were answered by Henri Ghéon who wrote :

" Is it fitting to regard as sacrilege the changing of the purpose of a piece of music ? The first culprit is the composer who did not explain to us the literary or artistic dream, in every case unconnected with music, which he wished to translate into pure music. I should not advise anyone

[1] *Le Figaro*, June 6th. 1910.

to imitate Bakst and Fokine in this, but I consider that the
manner in which they have translated Rimsky-Korsakov's
poem, without regard to the original plan, is perfectly
justifiable. This music had a certain significance but it
had a great many others, and, in a more general way,
without the aid of a synopsis or a picture, no music by itself
can express an idea or feeling, still less colour or form—
nothing but movement. The movements in *Schéhérazade*
are correct and that is sufficient."

M. D. Calvocoressi, the musical critic of the *Comœdia
Illustré*, replied in a similar strain :

" The suppression of one of the four movements is the
only thing that has taken place. We need not discuss the
question whether there ensued from this a break in the
musical balance ; there remains the question whether, if
at different moments in the music a new meaning be
attributed to them, the result be artistically false. I am
well aware that the negroes are massacred at the moment
when Rimsky-Korsakov's music refers to Sinbad's ship-
wreck, but I cannot help feeling envious of those whose
sense of rhythm and notes is so precise that any different
meaning is intolerable to them.

" How far are they from that German professor, both
learned and authoritative, who, in his analysis of
Schéhérazade, terms ' Shahryar's theme ' what another com-
mentator of no less merit styles ' sea theme,' with other
curiosities of the same kind ; from Johann Sebastian Bach
himself who accords to an identical piece of music the
duty of expressing in one case the pleasure of hunting, and
in another the religious fervour of a soul exalted by
prayer ! "[1]

VII

On the 24th of June there was a private rehearsal of
L'Oiseau de Feu. The next evening saw its first perfor-
mance, the programme being *Le Carnaval*, *L'Oiseau de Feu*,
Les Orientales, and the *Polovtsian Dances* from *Prince Igor*.
The new ballet was, as we have seen, the first work written
for ballet by Stravinsky. But legends associated with the

[1] July 1st, 1911.

Bird of Fire had inspired other national composers. Balakirev planned an opera of which the central figure was to be the Bird of Fire. Köstchei, the terrible ogre of Folkine's ballet, forms the subject and title of an opera by Rimsky-Korsakov ; this character again appears in a minor rôle in the same composer's opera-ballet *Mlada*.

The costumes and setting for *L'Oiseau de Feu* were designed by Golovin. The principal parts were allotted thus : T. Karsavina (*the Bird of Fire*), V. Fokina (*Tsarevna*), M. Fokine (*Ivan Tsarevich*) and E. Cecchetti (*Köstchei*).

* *
*

The ballet commences with an overture which soon creates an atmosphere of witchcraft, goblins, and attendant magic. The music has a peculiar timbre. There are low mutterings, mysterious long-drawn wails as of one unknown creature calling to another, the tramp of gnomes underground, strange rustlings, moans, the rumble of distant thunder, the music of a stream coursing over stones—and above all can be heard, at first faintly, then with increasing distinctness, the tremulous whirr of the wings of a bird soaring in circular flight.

When the curtain rises all is dark, a land of shadows, save only in the centre where, bathed in a circle of amber light, grows a tree, its branches laden with golden fruit. The music increases in volume and the scene lightens slightly to reveal the depths of a forest. Not a breath of air stirs in the trees. Presently a bird, gleaming with orange radiance, flashes across the background of foliage. Now it is possible to discern a high wall to the right, over which a youth in hunting-dress clambers. It is Ivan Tsarevich. In one hand he holds a crossbow with bolt ready in the slide, with the other he parts the bushes as he peers anxiously to right and left. The whirr of wings is heard and the Bird of Fire flits to the tree. The Prince raises his weapon, takes aim, and looses the bolt, but he misses and the startled bird flies away into the depths of the forest.

The Prince remains concealed and soon the bird returns to play amid the gleaming leaves of the magic tree. He approaches with stealthy steps and catches it in his arms. The bird struggles until exhausted, then offers him a golden feather for ransom. Ivan assents and allows it to go free. The scene grows lighter, and it is possible to see that through the trees runs a light palisade, ending in two gates through which is visible a flight of steps lost in shadow. Ivan is about to depart when a plaintive melody is heard and twelve maidens wind their way across a sloping eminence and down the steps. The Prince, amazed, steps into the shadow.

The gates open and the maidens go toward the tree where they are presently joined by another whose rich dress proclaims her rank. They shake the tree so that the apples fall to the ground and roll in all directions. The maidens career in pursuit, and each throws her prize high in the air to catch it and throw it to a companion. Ivan comes from his hiding-place and doffs his cap to them. But the leader of the maidens warns him to depart, for he is before the castle of Köstchei, an enchanter of mighty power, who captures all who trespass on his domains. The Prince, however, already in love with the maiden, wishes to stay.

Suddenly there sounds a discordant note which is repeated. The startled maidens run through the gates, which close after them. The Prince is about to take his departure when darkness descends and he is unable to find an outlet. He runs to and fro in terror, then turns to the gates and strives to open them. He shakes them. They fly open, the forest blazes with light, and down the eminence pours a motley horde of demons and goblins. They fall on the Prince and hold him fast, to await the coming of Köstchei.

The maidens come down the steps, then more guards, and finally the enchanter himself. He glares at his victim and strives to cast a spell upon him, but Ivan remembers the golden feather and waves it aloft. To his aid flies the glorious Bird of Fire, who scatters his enemies and begins a dance of swiftly increasing measure. The demons are compelled to follow her until, exhausted, they sink to the ground and fall into a deep slumber. The Bird of Fire bids Ivan take the chief of the maidens to a place of safety, then shows him a root which marks the base of a hollow tree. He crawls inside to reappear with an iron-bound casket.

He raises the lid and withdraws an enormous egg, which he throws into the air and catches as it falls, while Köstchei, who knows that it contains his soul, trembles with fear and apprehension. In desperation he clutches at the precious object, but Ivan dashes it to the ground. There is a deafening crash and darkness falls.

Presently the stage lightens, showing the palisade broken asunder while Köstchei, his court, and the Bird of Fire have vanished. In their place is a group of young men dressed richly, who pay homage to Ivan. Down the steps comes a beautiful Princess, the maiden to whom he pledged his troth, and in her train a group of nobles and fair dames, now freed from enchantment by the death of Köstchei. They are followed by a procession of pages, who bear in their midst a crown, sceptre, and ermine robe. Ivan is invested with these symbols of power and the assembly acclaim him as their deliverer and sovereign lord.

* *
*

It will be easy to perceive, from the review which we shall presently quote, that this ballet was regarded as a triumph of Fokine's choregraphic genius. The miming was natural and convincing, far removed from the conventionalized and meaningless gestures of the traditional ballet. The dances were ingenious and varied. The *pas de deux* between the Prince and the Bird of Fire, with its many charming passages, the graceful dance of the maidens, the weird, grotesque movements of the demons—all delighted the Parisians to the full.

The first performance, however, contained many trials for the *maître de ballet*. The ballet was not completed before the company arrived in Paris, and, although Fokine held many daily rehearsals in order to mould it into shape, he felt that it would not be ready by the date fixed. He urged Diaghilev to postpone the ballet, but, as the director

did not wish to disappoint the public, it was decided to
risk its being ready in time. It was a nerve-wracking
period for Fokine, who was oppressed with gloomy fore-
bodings that all his efforts would be doomed to failure on
account of insufficient rehearsals ; there were many times
when he gave way to tears. Even at the dress rehearsal
many of the costumes and properties were not ready, the
lighting was poor, and the apparatus designed to carry
Karsavina who, as the Bird of Fire, had to appear to
fly across the sky background, did not work freely, but
creaked and grated the whole time. Nevertheless, the
whole company were intensely interested in the new ballet
and loyally supported its creator, so that the performance,
instead of being a failure, was a glorious success.

Here are some of the opinions of the French critics :

" This ballet, conceived and arranged by the eminent
choreographer Fokine . . . evokes and embodies all the
picturesque, strange, and invincible charm of the tales of
Slav mythology. It is displayed in a sumptuous and
novel *décor*, the work of Golovin, and the costumes are of
a refined and unprecedented variety. In short, the whole
effect, like that of *Schéhérazade*, is destined to surprise,
captivate, and transport."[1]

" I shall not describe the story, it is not sensual, but
simply artless and wonderful. It introduces us to a fable
purer and more intellectual than that of *Schéhérazade*. It
does not arrest at first glance, but impresses gradually and
it is impossible to be wearied by it. The chirping tones,
the caressing vivacity of the melody, the nightmare of
forms, the delirium of the dance, the charming naïvety of
Prince Ivan (how he deserves to be rescued) plunge us again,
by means of the most refined art, into the ecstasy of the
stories of our childhood."[2]

" The management of the Russian ballet has just set the
seal on its season by the most complete, the most beautiful,
spectacle it has yet afforded us. And this beauty is not of

[1] *Le Figaro*, June 24th, 1910.

[2] Ghéon (Henri) *" Propos Divers sur le Ballet Russe."* Nouvelle
Revue Française. Quoted Svetlov. *Op. cit.*

a transitory nature which procures only momentary pleasure, it is invested with a much higher and rarer significance. *L'Oiseau de Feu* for a moment conveyed the illusion of being a masterpiece, reflection will doubtless lessen our enthusiasm of yesterday, but it will likewise afford us the strongest assurance that the choregraphic story of MM. Fokine and Stravinsky heralds an entirely new direction for the art of dancing. Prior to *L'Oiseau de Feu* we have seen many ballets, pleasing and brilliant, adorned with interesting or mediocre music, sometimes of a high value, but always subordinated to the exigencies of a discreet tradition. *L'Oiseau de Feu* is perhaps the first which is entirely free from these fetters ; the descriptive music, the setting, and the choregraphic realisation, all contribute to the interest. And if ever the manifestations of Russian art have provided a lesson, the performance of yesterday is certainly the highest proof of it, not so much in the matter of detail—although always captivating—as detail, but by the spirit which animates it and by the problem of choregraphic æsthetics which it raises."[1]

[1] *Le Figaro,* June 27th, 1910.

[Photo : Jaeger, Copenhagen

SCENE FROM " SCHÉHÉRAZADE," AS PRESENTED AT THE ROYAL THEATRE, COPENHAGEN
V. FOKINE   M. FOKINE

[Photo: Studio des Capucines, Paris

SCENE FROM "LE SPECTRE DE LA ROSE"

I

ON the company's return to St. Petersburg, Diaghilev
decided to prepare further novelties. These were *Le
Spectre de la Rose, Narcisse, Petrouchka,* and *Sadko (Le
Royaume Sous-marin).*

The theme of the first-named was suggested by the
poet J. L. Vaudoyer, during the company's first visit to
Paris. It is an adaptation of Gautier's little poem, the
subject of which is the evocation of the spirit of a rose
given to a young girl at a ball. The dance was set to
Weber's well-known piece *L'Invitation à la Valse.* Fokine's
intention was to use Nijinsky's elevation to create a poetical
picture of the rose-coloured sprite so that the dance executed
by the sleeping girl—a new theme in ballet—which was
taken by Karsavina, afforded a charming contrast to the
energetic movements of the male dancer who represented
the spirit of the rose.

Narcisse has a curious history. It will be remembered
that Fokine's first *scenario,* which he submitted to the
management of the Imperial Theatres, was based on the
Daphnis and Chloe of Longus. As we know, it was never
produced. But Fokine had a particular affection for this
theme and when Maurice Ravel expressed a wish to compose a ballet, he gave him his synopsis for *Daphnis et
Chloé.* Bakst prepared a design for the scenery which
represented a leafy glade, at one side of which stood a
group of rocks on which were carved the figures of three
nymphs. But when it was found that Ravel would not
have time to compose the music to enable the ballet to
be given at the next Paris season, Diaghilev commissioned
Tcherepnine to compose the music for a ballet in the Grecian
style ; this was *Narcisse,* the theme being the outcome of
a collaboration between the composer and Bakst. The

69

scenery used was that designed for *Daphnis et Chloé*. Fokine found it difficult to work on *Narcisse*, as he felt it contained so much of what he had intended for the earlier ballet, on which he had meditated for so many years.

Some time towards the latter part of the year 1910 Stravinsky began to write a suite of short pieces for the piano, the themes of which were intended to suggest the attributes of different types of dolls, such as a toy Dancer, a Moor, and a Petrouchka. Diaghilev was very impressed by this composition and asked Stravinsky if he could not devise a ballet in the same style. Benois was called in to collaborate with him on the general outline of the story, and soon afterwards Fokine began to work on the mime and dances. He did not collaborate with Benois to any extent. He was given the score and a rough draft of the *scenario*, and developed the details mostly from listening to the music, particularly in the case of the action that takes place in Petrouchka's cell and in the luxurious apartment of the Moor.

At the same time, Fokine composed a ballet to a scene taken from Rimsky-Korsakov's opera *Sadko*. It was called *Le Royaume Sous-marin* (*The Kingdom under the Sea*). This was presented first at the Constanza Theatre, Rome, where the company went to give a series of performances during the Exhibition held in that city. The rehearsals of *Petrouchka*, as the doll ballet was entitled, were continued during their stay.

On Friday, June 2nd, the company left Rome for Paris. The base selected was the Théâtre du Chatelet. The news of the arrival of the Diaghilev Company, which had been announced in the press several days previously, was received with the greatest interest, and every box and stall for the first performance was quickly booked. The season was to last a fortnight, with a complete change of programme for each week. The programme of the first performance, given on June 6th, was *Le Carnaval*, with Karsavina, Fokina, Schollar, Nijinska, and Nijinsky, Bolm, Cecchetti, Kussov, and Semenov; *Narcisse*, with Karsavina, Fedorova, Fokina, Schollar, Tcherepanova, and

Nijinsky ; *Le Spectre de la Rose,* with Karsavina and
Nijinsky ; and *Le Royaume Sous-marin,* an *ensemble* ballet.

II

The scene of *Narcisse* represents a sylvan glade overhung
with a dense mass of foliage, great drooping branches
depending from invisible trees as if weary from the heat.
In the distance, almost hidden by the wealth of verdure,
can be seen the outline of a natural bridge formed of moss-
grown rock. At the right, surrounded by a low, grassy
bank, bathed in the red glow of the rising sun, gleams a
silent pool.

As the light grows stronger there depart a little band
of grotesque wood sprites who, content to sport till dawn,
fear to stay longer lest the coming of humans should bring
them harm. The distant sound of music, which rises and
falls in a brilliant cascade of notes, heralds the arrival of a
number of Boetians who amuse themselves with dances
in honour of the gods of the woods and fields. Soon
they are joined by some Bacchantes who offer gifts to the
goddess Pomona and dance in her praise.

A song is borne on the breeze. It is the voice of Narcissus who enters, radiant and happy, pursued by two
enamoured nymphs. The merry company give place to
him, and, in response to the request of his friends, he dances
for their delight. The dance is interrupted by the arrival
of Echo who is in love with Narcissus, and to whom she
declares her passion. But the two nymphs, jealous of
their rival, warn him that his love cannot be returned,
since Echo can only repeat the last words and gestures
of others and cannot express or feel anything herself.
At this, Narcissus forsakes her company and yields to the
attractions and entreaties of the nymphs, who bear him
away in triumph, while the company disappear into the
depths of the forest.

Echo, left alone in her sorrow, falls to weeping and
prays to the gods to avenge so unkind a slight. The light
grows dim and all is silent. Echo's prayer is answered
and the gods decree that Narcissus shall love where he can

never hope his love to be returned. Narcissus returns, moody and ill at ease, and, ignoring Echo, climbs on to the bank. Then, cupping his hand, he bends over the pool so that he may fill it with water with which to quench his thirst. But, no sooner does he incline his head, than he sees his image reflected in the placid waters. Astonished at such exquisite beauty he stretches out his hands to embrace the vision, but, as he touches the surface of the pool, it resolves into a hundred ripples and disappears.

In despair, he rises to his feet, while Echo again entreats his love. He turns towards her and then again glances at the pool. The ripples have subsided and he beholds the lovely image once more. He falls on his knees and watches it in ecstasy. The shadows fall thickly and the insects begin their evening songs. Echo, seeing her efforts fruitless, draws slowly away, mounts the bridge, and is transformed into a rock, to repeat for ever the sounds which shall disturb her solitude.

Narcissus, still absorbed in contemplation, watches with horror his image become more and more obscured as the darkness grows in intensity. Almost imperceptibly he is swallowed up and there rises from the centre of the pool a single narcissus flower. With dusk, the wood sprites return and view with surprise the golden bloom.

**
*

This beautiful creation was far removed from *Eunice,* Fokine's first essay in the antique style. While the latter was not completely free from the pseudo antiques of the old ballet, *Narcisse* made no concessions to tradition. This tale, so full of sadness, was presented with a remarkable simplicity and economy of gesture. The dances, poses, and groups showed a careful study of Greek sculpture and vase paintings. The quaint movements and strange attitudes of the wood sprites were contrasted with the gay dances of the Boetians and Bacchantes, thus affording additional strength to the severely classic movements accorded to Echo and Narcissus. It is difficult to forget Echo's imitation of the gestures of Narcissus, and that lovely movement of her arm where her grief is symbolised by the raising of her violet scarf to hide her eyes bedewed with tears.

Benois declared that, in his opinion, *Narcisse*, more than any other ballet, expressed most the ideals which Fokine had at heart. A critic said of the first performance : " *Narcisse* obtained a triumphal success shared by the *maître de ballet*, Fokine, whose dances are admirably arranged, Nijinsky, who surpasses the renown of Vestris, Mmes. Fokina, Nijinska, and, finally, the delicious Karsavina in the character of Echo."

III

The scenery designed by Leon Bakst for *Le Spectre de la Rose* is a treasure of Victorian simplicity and primness. It represents a young girl's bedroom. The room, octagonal in shape, is pure white, except where the walls are covered with a deep blue paper on which stands out, in sharp relief, a simple floral design, also in white. Between the two windows is placed a sofa covered in blue and white chintz, at the side of which is a round table, on which stands a bowl of roses. To the right, situated in an alcove, is a small wooden bed, the sheets of which are thrown back as if awaiting to enfold their dainty mistress. At the foot is a comfortable leather arm-chair and her sketching-easel. On the left side is her dressing-table with looking-glass and powder-puff carefully arranged. Everything indicates the neatness and simplicity of the owner. In the left and right back corners are tall french windows thrown wide open to reveal a garden with high clusters of rose bushes almost covered with pink and red blossoms. Overhead can be seen the warm blue sky of a summer's evening, and through the open windows streams the moonlight, flecking the floor with bright patches of green and yellow.

From the garden comes a gentle breeze laden with the fragrance of roses, and into the room steps a young girl, sweet and demure in her high-cut ball-dress of creamy white, over which is lightly fastened a little cloak. In her hand she gently holds a rose, fearful lest her tiny fingers should crumple its fragile beauty. She raises it to her

73

lips and imprints on it a loving kiss. What tender secrets does it hold, this lover's gift? She gazes upon it with downcast eyes. Surely it is not wrong to be loved? Her lips quiver and seem to murmur his name. She glances around the room, so friendly, so dear to her, with all its innocent treasures. Now that her face is upraised how tired she looks. Perhaps, little accustomed to worldly pleasures, the excitement of the ball has proved too great for her. She throws off her wrap and walks slowly to her arm-chair. She sinks into it with a sigh of content, her eyes close, and in a few moments she is fast asleep. Her limp hands fall and through her fingers the rose slips, caresses her dress, and glides to the floor.

The music quickens to a rapturous movement and through the open window alights the object of her dream, the spirit of the rose. With what joy, with what abandon, does he dance, blown hither and thither like a rose petal in the wind.

At his magic touch she is spirited out of her chair to join him in the ever-quickening, soothing melody of the waltz. How high she leaps, yet so gracefully that it seems as if she, too, had forsaken her mortal body. Together they float through the still air, impelled everywhere by the fairy-like touch of his hand. Then the music slowly dies away and ceases. A moment and she is again in her chair, her features still calm in repose, unruffled, as if what had just transpired was but an elfin touch of our imagination. Bending over her for a brief instant, the rose-coloured sprite disappears through the open window just as the first rays of dawn trace curious shadows on the wall.

The maiden stirs, and, smoothing her sleep-laden eyes, looks around her as if what was in truth but a dream were reality. The room is empty. Still doubting, she bends and picks up her precious rose. Then she remembers, her face lights up in a sad half-smile, and as she presses the rose to her bosom the curtain falls.

* *
*

This dance is certainly one of the most poetical of all Fokine's creations. It illustrates exactly his contention that the technique of the classical ballet should be employed only where it is applicable. *Le Spectre de la Rose* is a classical *pas de deux* and Nijinksy's wonderful elevation was employed in such a manner that his leaps and bounds seemed the embodiment of grace and ease, the natural attributes of an ethereal being, and not the product of an extraordinary technique.

The composition is a choregraphic poem of rare beauty. As Svetlov remarks : " There is nothing superfluous in this ballet. Everything is fragrant with subtle and delicate charm. The ballet contains no pantomime and no dramatic subject. It is ripe with the pure romantic classicism with which Marie Taglioni conquered Europe and America."

Robert Brussel, reviewing the first performance of the new season, declared : " Among the whole programme one work stands quite apart by virtue of its charm and perfection. I do not know whether Théophile Gautier's fable accords exactly with the simple intentions Weber had in mind when writing *L'Invitation à la Valse*, one aspect only need be considered : the performance, and that is exquisite." Another critic wrote : " *The Spectre de la Rose* was cheered to the echo. This duet mimed and danced by Karsavina and Nijinsky cast over the public a spell of overpowering charm and compelled their admiration." This ballet achieved a furore wherever it was given. On a later occasion when it was danced at an official charity performance held at the Grand Opera, Paris, which realised over 100,000 francs, it achieved so overwhelming a success that in response to the clamours of the audience for an encore, the whole was repeated—an unprecedented event for Paris.

IV

The ballet, *Le Royaume Sous-marin*, was Fokine's first essay in the production of opera-ballet. The vocal part was sung by Mme. Stepanova-Chevtchenko and Mm. Issatchenko and Zaporojetz. The dances were entirely *en masse*, there were neither solos nor principal dancers.

This is the theme of the opera. Sadko, a poor but spirited

minstrel, wagers his head against the riches of the Novgorod merchants that he will catch golden fish in a certain Lake Ilmen. He wins as the result of aid afforded him by the Sea King's daughter, who is enamoured of him. He embarks on one of the fleet of ships that have become his, but a great storm arises and it is decided by the company to propitiate the Sea King by offering him one of their number. Lots are drawn and this duty falls on Sadko, who throws himself into the sea.

He descends into the realm of the Sea King who invites him to play to the court on his *gusli*, which he does with such goodwill that soon the King and his subjects begin to dance. Their movements grow wilder and wilder and set the whole sea in motion so that a terrible storm arises. But St. Nicholas, fearing for the safety of the mariners, causes the *gusli* to fall to the ground, commands Sadko to return home, and transforms the Sea King's daughter into the River Volkov on which the town of Novgorod stands. The scene " The Kingdom under the Sea " deals with Sadko's entrance and departure from the Sea King's domain, and ends a little differently in that Sadko himself breaks the strings of his instrument and makes his escape to the upper world, taking the King's daughter with him as his bride.

* *
*

The costumes and scenery designed by Boris Anisfeld are full of a fantastic beauty. The dancers represent Sea Currents, Sea Plants, Sea Horses, and many varieties of fish. Though first produced in Rome the ballet was not fully completed until the Paris season. The company employed was a large one ; there were some seventy dancers and many supers who did not dance but were placed in groups and performed a few simple, rhythmic movements so that they made a plastic contrast to the ballet. The dances contained many original movements suggestive of swimming and water in motion. There were special movements for the hands, one particularly interesting which conveyed the impression of a splash of water. The ballet was very well received.

76

[*Photo : Studio des Capucines, Paris*

SCENE FROM " LE ROYAUME SOUS-MARIN "

[*Photo : Studio des Capucines, Paris*

SCENE FROM " PETROUCHKA " (SCENE I)

" Sadko," wrote one critic, " is the wonder of wonders. This ballet, sung by a chorus and at the same time mimed and danced by the whole *corps de ballet*, is certainly, both as regards setting and colour, the most artistic performance which the Russian ballet has given in Paris during the last five (*sic*) years. We heartily congratulate the *maître de ballet*, Fokine, the great creator of this series of remarkable performances."

The ballet, however, did not remain in the repertory for long as Diaghilev did not have so large a company in the subsequent seasons. It was, however, given at St. Petersburg on the 10th of March, 1912, at a charity performance held in aid of the Literary Fund. It was purchased by the management but not added to the repertory, because someone raised objection to Anisfeld's scenery being used in an opera decorated by other painters.

V

The first of the second group of performances began on June 13th. It consisted of *Petrouchka*, *Le Spectre de la Rose*, and *Schéhérazade*. Between the first two ballets the orchestra played a symphonic *entr'acte*, Rimsky-Korsakov's " La Bataille de Kerjenetz," for which a decorative drop-curtain was painted by Roehrich.

Petrouchka, styled a Burlesque Ballet in Four Scenes, was composed, as we have seen, by Stravinsky; the setting and costumes were designed by Benois. The ballet was nearly ready when the company came to Paris, only the dances for the principals remained to be finished. Fokine had to compose under difficulties. The flats which compose Petrouchka's cell were set up on the stage and the choreographer taught Nijinsky his part; but all the time workmen were passing through the joins in the scenery, and the sounds of an opera class at rehearsal were plainly audible.

* *
*

The scene represents the Admiralty Square, St. Petersburg, in the year 1830, during the revels which take place on the last three days before Lent, *Maslenitsa*—Butter Week

—a period of peasant holiday and debauch before the abstinence of the forty days. Two curtains are used in the performance of this ballet ; the first is the usual barrier between the audience and the dancers, the second is that which screens the interior of the Showman's booth from both the real and the stage audience.

Prior to the raising of the curtain there is a brief overture extraordinarily descriptive of the sounds of a fair—the bustle of a seething mass of people bent on amusement, the raucous invitations shouted by the owners of side-shows, the jargon of noise produced by innumerable instruments all playing a different tune, while, above all, can be heard the grinding melody of a combined mechanical organ and roundabout.

The scene depicts a fair held in mid-winter. To the left is a booth hung with red and white striped curtains upon the top of which is a yellow boarded platform. Here, sheltered under a coarse blue awning, is an old man who calls attention to the length of his beard, and two gypsies who entreat onlookers to have their fortunes told. To the right, backing on to the side of a wooden hut, is a collection of stalls loaded with sweets and trinkets. In the centre is another booth, rectangular in shape, the contents of which are screened by a blue curtain. Behind loom the top of a roundabout and the misty outline of the Admiralty spire. Over the snow-covered ground comes and goes a multi-coloured throng, laughing, shouting, dancing, as full of fun as can be. In turn they make way for a band of peasants, who noisily stamp to the lively strains of a concertina, and a street dancer who steps to the accompaniment of a hurdy-gurdy. Suddenly, two drummers emerge from the interior of the centre booth, and commence to beat a vigorous tattoo. A whistle sounds and the bearded head of a showman appears through the curtain. He steps forth, then, striding to the side of the booth, causes the curtain to fly back revealing three compartments, in each of which grotesquely sprawls a puppet. The first is a Moor, the second a Ballerina, the third Petrouchka. At a signal from the showman they break into a quick, automatic dance and presently come out of the booth into the snow. The crowd applauds heartily. Suddenly the puppets collapse to the ground and all is dark.

The second scene shows Petrouchka's cell, a triangular apartment of deep black lightly powdered with silver stars, at the left of which is a low double door. Presently this flies open and Petrouchka is impelled through the opening by the Showman's cruel boot. He tries in vain to escape from his prison. Again the door opens and the Ballerina enters, to him a figure of surpassing beauty. He seeks to gain her favour by an exhibition of wonderful leaps, but he is coldly received and the Ballerina departs. Again he tries to find an outlet, tears at the wall, then falls headlong to the ground. The light vanishes.

The third scene presents the home of the Moor, a very luxurious apartment decorated with red wall-paper patterned with gigantic palm-trees. In the centre stands a divan upon which the Moor sprawls, playing with a cocoa-nut. Then he tries to break the nut with his scimitar and, failing to do so, believes it to be a fetish. He prays to it, when the door opens and the Ballerina enters carrying a toy trumpet, with which she dances. The Moor drops the cocoanut and watches her with delight. Presently he pulls her on to his lap when the door again opens and Petrouchka appears. The guilty pair separate and the Moor chases Petrouchka, and eventually dispatches him through the door with a kick. Triumphant, he pulls the Ballerina again on his knee. All is dark.

The fourth scene shows the fair again ; but time has passed, the sky is darkening and nightfall is imminent. Some sightseers are preparing to depart while a few more boisterous spirits, several coachmen, invite some nurse-maids to dance, an attempt which is frustrated by the ladies' escorts. Now the nursemaids decide to dance among themselves. Meanwhile the crowd is distracted by new arrivals : a performing bear, a vendor of ribbons, a merchant with a gypsy girl on each arm. The coachmen begin a lively dance in which the girls join until interrupted by a group of revellers with their faces concealed by grotesque masks. The scene grows darker and now a terrible commotion is heard in the booth where the puppets live.

The curtain is violently agitated and out leaps Petrouchka followed by the Moor with upraised scimitar ; at his heels runs the frightened Ballerina. With a vicious sweep of his blade the Moor fells Petrouchka to the ground, then runs away, accompanied by the Ballerina. A crowd quickly collects and a policeman is summoned who returns with the Showman. He seizes the corpse and points out its stuffed body and wooden limbs. The crowd, relieved, departs homewards, while the Showman drags the useless puppet behind him. Suddenly there is an unearthly shriek and on the top of the booth appears the head and shoulders of the wraith of Petrouchka. The Showman looks upward, starts back in terror, drops his burden and flees.

* *
*

If ever any ballet had the right to be acclaimed a masterpiece, it is certainly *Petrouchka*. It is impossible to describe the vivid sense of life which animates the whole. The crowd is quite extraordinary, it does not march methodically to and fro like soldiers at review in the manner of the old ballet ; the people jostle and push each other, struggle to obtain the best view of the peep-show, exchange greetings, compare opinions on the merits of the rival street-dancers, banter the proprietors of the stalls—one may see this ballet a score of times and yet find some new by-play which in the wealth of various incidents offered had hitherto passed unnoticed. But, though everything is apparently so spontaneous, we know that the slightest gesture has been prescribed by the choregrapher. Imagine the thought expended in working out the infinite number of details and then combining them to form one homogeneous picture !

The steps for the dolls are worked out with the same loving care ; there are clumsy steps and florid movements for the Moor ; dainty, *pizzicato* steps for the Ballerina ; and stiff, wooden gestures for the hapless Petrouchka. Yet, though all the movements of these puppets are essentially doll-like, by some cunning art Fokine has succeeded

[*Photo: Studio des Capucines, Paris*

SCENE FROM " PETROUCHKA " (SCENE II)

SCENE FROM " PETROUCHKA " (SCENE III)

in investing them with a certain mystic symbolism. The spectator, from his first introduction to them, feels that for all their expressionless faces, their bodies of saw-dust, they possess a soul. The dances, too, are full of variety and national character. Who can forget the hand-claps and lusty rhythmic stamps of the fat coachmen, the semi-stupid movements of the nurses, the frenzied dances of the gypsies —red and orange skirts flashing, hips swaying voluptu-ously, arms flung aloft, fingers snapping, feet shuffling ; all executed with a fine devilry—and the terrifying gestures of the masked revellers who pretend to frighten the women. *Petrouchka*, as the eminent critic Vuillemin stated, " is a miracle of choregraphic art."

During the first performance Stravinsky expressed his gratitude to Fokine, and Benois complimented him on having been so successful in grasping the human drama in the ballet, but he did not approve of Fokine's production of the dance by the wet-nurses which occurs in the last scene. He felt that it should have been popular, gay, and pretty. Fokine, on the contrary, gave the dance an animalistic character because, to him, there is something unnatural in the spectacle of a woman who, in return for money, gives her own milk to another's child.

W. A. Propert, in his book, *The Russian Ballet in Western Europe*, referring to Nijinsky's performance of Petrouchka, states : " The part is all his own, for Fokine had given him perfect freedom in the making of it." This is not true, and must be corrected. In every ballet produced by Fokine, he creates every pose, step, gesture, and ex-pression, whether for the principal artistes or those of lesser degree. Curiously enough, Nijinsky had great difficulty in remembering the various movements set for his part, and Fokine, at the dancer's request, prompted him from behind the scenery at the first performance, during the whole episode in Petrouchka's room.

VI

On Fokine's return to St. Petersburg he was com-missioned by the management of the Imperial Theatres to arrange the dances for a revival of Gluck's opera, *Orpheus*. The general production was entrusted to Vsevelod Meyerhold. The setting and costumes were designed by A. Golovine who had been engaged on these for some time.

Fokine was very enthusiastic over the scene of the Underworld in the second act, which he planned so that when the curtain was raised the audience saw the stage filled with inanimate bodies. The artistes forming the groups were posed in the most unnatural positions, so that they appeared to be contorted with pain and suffering agonising torments. Some were seen clinging to rocks, others hanging over precipices, which latter were represented by open trap-doors. When the chorus sang : " Who is the mortal one now drawing near to this region of gloominess, bold to intrude on these awful bodies ? " the whole mass of bodies made one slow movement which conveyed the impression of an enormous monster raising itself in a menacing attitude. There was just this one slow movement, the pose was retained for an instant, then the mass melted away to form new groups.

The whole ballet company, the male and female chorus, the whole theatre school, and many hundred supers took part in this movement. Those by the trap-doors clambered up on the rocks, while others crawled down, still others crawled across the stage. Everyone seemed doomed to a restless movement, a vain eternal effort to seek peace. When these dances were rehearsed in the practice-room the rocks were contrived out of chairs and tables, but even under these conditions the effect was ghastly in the extreme. All the artistes were very engrossed and excited.

When the rehearsals were transferred to the stage, Meyerhold asked Fokine to go through the whole act with the chorus and those that were taking part in it. He was glad to assist in this task, as from the beginning he had considered the ballet in its relation to the opera and not as a separate part of it. He was therefore delighted to endeavour to realise his principle of uniting the work of all the artistes so that the audience should be unable to tell where the ballet began and the vocal chorus ended. The dance of the Furies and that of the Spirits were evolved naturally out of this plastic group.

The vocal chorus was no less enthusiastic than the dancers, for when Fokine (noticing that some of the former had to sing in the most uncomfortable positions, so that they were hanging head downwards, kneeling or clasping each other) wished to alter the poses so that they should be easier, one and all begged him not to change anything, promising to do all that was required of them.

Later he was asked to produce other scenes. In the first act, where Orpheus sheds tears over the tomb of Eurydice, he staged a large group symbolical of grief. This contained little movement, the mourning cloaks were removed and then put on again. Then there were a few ritual movements when flowers are laid on the grave and the chorus moves slowly and sadly away. Fokine also staged the dances and groups of the Blessed Spirits in the scene of Elysium, together with the long mimed scene between Orpheus and Eurydice, as the former's movements depended on those composed for the chorus and ballet.

In the last scene, which is concerned with the joyful surprise and reunion of Orpheus and Eurydice, he introduced *amorini* suggesting the groups in Versailles. These were danced by the smallest girls in the school, some of whom carried white roses. He also arranged the dances for the artistes, both male and female.

The production was performed at the Maryinsky Theatre on the 21st of December, 1911, for the benefit of the artistes of the chorus of the Imperial Opera. The programme stated : " Opera produced by V. Meyerhold and M. Fokine," but the chorus paid tribute to the part Fokine took in this production by presenting a wreath to Golovine and himself.

Unfortunately, the opera was unlucky. It was received with tremendous success the first season, but could not be revived the following years as on each occasion Fokine happened to be abroad. Then, during the War, it could not be included in the repertory owing to its being the work of a German composer.

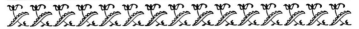

CHAPTER NINE
PRODUCTION OF "ISLAMEY," "PAPILLONS," "LE DIEU BLUE," "THAMAR," AND "DAPHNIS ET CHLOÉ"

I

DURING 1912 Fokine produced five new ballets : *Islamey. Papillons, Le Dieu Bleu, Thamar,* and *Daphnis et Chloé,* The first two were produced on the 10th of March at a charity performance given at the Maryinsky Theatre in aid of the Literary Fund.

Both *Islamey* and *Papillons* are, in a sense, reflections of his earlier ballets *Schéhérazade* and *Le Carnaval.* Fokine wished to show in St. Petersburg a ballet in his Eastern manner, but, since *Schéhérazade* could not be given, as Rimsky-Korsakov's widow prohibited the performance of the symphony in Russia when associated with ballet, he thought of using Balakirev's "Islamey" as the basis for a ballet in a similar style. At first the composer's heir, S. M. Liapunov, protested against such profanation, but finally gave his consent, and, moreover, agreed to orchestrate the piece, which was written for the piano only.

The theme of the ballet, also taken from *The Thousand and One Nights,* is based on the story of the young King of the Black Islands. The king's wife gives her husband a cup of wine which she has drugged with bhang. But he has been advised of her plot and only pretends to drink the wine and fall asleep. The wife then conceals her husband behind a curtain and welcomes her lover, who is a negro. At the height of their love-making the king emerges from behind the curtain and slays the lover. The wife is so terrified at her husband's unexpected appearance that she throws herself out of the window and falls over a precipice.

The scene, which was designed by B. Anisfeld, represents an Eastern harem, the colour scheme being a wonderful blending of gold and purple. The dances, which are very passionate during the love scene, change

Photo : Raoul Barba, Monte Carlo

SCENE FROM " PETROUCHKA " (SCENE IV)
(*As presented by Les Ballets de Monte Carlo*)

MICHEL FOKINE AS DAPHNIS IN "DAPHNIS ET CHLOÉ"

on the king's entry to an expression of fear. *Islamey* is full of dances, movements, mimed scenes, and brilliant colours, but it is short and lasts only seven minutes ; impression succeeds impression with lightning rapidity so that it is necessary to see the ballet many times to appreciate it to the full.

The chief characters were taken as follows : Gerdt (*The King*), Karsavina (*The King's Wife*), and Fokine (*The Lover*). As a result of the success of the production, *Islamey* was immediately added to the repertory. The first public performance took place on the 15th of December, 1913, when the parts of the Wife and Lover were interpreted by V. Fokina and B. Romanov.

II

Papillons is danced to Schumann's music of the same name ; it is a set of twelve little pianoforte pieces dating from his early days at Heidelberg. The meaning of these is to be found in the penultimate chapter of Jean Paul's *Flegeljahre* in which a ball is described. It was orchestrated for the purpose of the ballet by N. Tcherepnine. The costumes were designed by Bakst, the setting by M. Dobuzhinsky.

* *
*

The scene represents the park attached to a mansion. The background is formed by a mass of foliage which parts in the centre where stands a statue set in a small domed temple. Through the opening can be seen the waters of a lake, and the dark silhouette of trees on the opposite bank. The foreground is flanked on each side by a circular domed building. The whole scene is bathed in moonlight.

The theme by Fokine is simple and, like that of *Le Carnaval*, placed in an 1830 setting. It is a Carnival night and a melancholy Pierrot wanders in the park. A group of girls dressed in yellow crinolines, with little wings attached to their shoulders, enter and dance round him. Pierrot is entranced and believing them to be butterflies seeks to attract them with a candle-flame. He succeeds in capturing

85

the prettiest, but he handles her so roughly that her wings break off and she sinks to the ground, dead. The young girl's companions come on the scene, lift up the butterfly, and carry her off in a sad procession. Pierrot, full of grief, finds the wings and entreats the girl's friends to try and revive his sweetheart. They succeed in re-attaching the wings and the young girl comes to life. He is happy again and all dance a wedding dance round Pierrot and his beloved.

Suddenly a clock strikes to proclaim the end of Carnival. The girls disappear to return walking decorously and accompanied by their chaperons and servants. The last of the guests to depart is a young masked girl escorted by a gentleman. Pierrot looks at her wonderingly. As she passes she turns her head towards him, half raises her mask, and smiles. Pierrot, seeing that he has been tricked, remains staring after her, overcome with the bitterness of his fate. He turns, sways, and falls headlong to the ground, his body shaken with the intensity of his grief.

* *
*

Papillons is a charming, ingenuous composition, delicate and fragile as a butterfly's wing. The groups, the miming, the *pas de deux*, and the scene of the death and reanimation of the butterfly are full of that poetry and tender lyricism characteristic of Fokine's work in this vein, but the impression afforded is slight and the piece naturally suffers from being a repetition of style. The principal characters were interpreted thus : Karsavina (*First Young Girl*) and Fokine (*Pierrot*).

III

The next three ballets were given during the Paris Season at the Théâtre du Chatelet. The first of these performances, given on the 13th of May, consisted of *Le Dieu Bleu*, *L'Oiseau de Feu*, *Le Spectre de la Rose*, and the *Polovtsian Dances* from *Prince Igor*. In *Le Dieu Bleu*, Fokine desired to give dances quite unlike those in his other ballets. He wished to use the angular poses of the limbs, the childishly-bent head, the turned-up palms and curved fingers characteristic of Hindu sculpture. The music was composed by Reynaldo Hahn, the theme by Jean Cocteau and Frederic de Madrazzo. The setting and costumes were designed by Leon Bakst.

* *
*

The scene represents a shrine concealed from the vulgar gaze by high cliffs. The background is formed by one huge rock, coloured deep orange. From the centre of the base of this rock grows a dense mass of foliage crowned by four gigantic heads hewn out of stone, which serve as symbols of the mighty deity worshipped by the natives. A greenish-brown cliff forms the right-hand side of the scene ; at its base writhe four immense serpents of a strange orange hue, speckled with black spots.

At the left hand is another cliff of similar colour, but where its outer surface has crumbled away, there gleam pieces of orange rock. In the front and side of this cliff are cut two doors, the first high and narrow, the second low and wide. There is a fissure between this cliff and the orange rock guarded by massive gates. Overhead glows the deep blue sky of an Indian night. High up in the firmament are little groups of scintillating stars, below them glows a deep rose lantern. To the centre of the scene at the back is a deep rock-girt pool in which the sacred lotus floats, and bending over the rim with neck outstretched is a sacred tortoise drinking of the holy water.

First enters a long procession of priests and attendants, followed by two stalwart Hindus with materials for a fire. This is lighted and while the novice who is to be made a priest humbles himself before it, the High Priest offers up prayers for the success of the ceremony. Fruit offerings and bowls for water from the sacred pool are brought in by further attendants. Some girls bring in a goat for the sacrifice. Together they perform the ceremony of obeisance prescribed for the occasion. As the rites proceed a dance is performed by three young women who each support on their shoulders a gorgeously-tailed peacock. As they turn and twist, so the beautiful tails sweep the ground. Now wild-eyed fakirs arrive who lash themselves into a state of religious frenzy until at last they drop from sheer weariness.

The ceremony concluded, the newly-ordained priest is clad in a long white robe, the outward sign of his office. Then the priest, taking him by the hand, presents him to the approving onlookers. As he passes all bow the head save a young girl who, leaning far forward, peers eagerly into his face as if to fathom his most inward thoughts. The young priest meets her passionate gaze and blushes deeply.

Only now is he conscious of what he has forsaken in his accursed ambition for office. No more can he clasp her to his breast as of old. He is vowed to chastity. He hesitates, then, composing himself, follows the high priest. But the ordeal is not ended for he must pass a second time before the audience. Again he meets his beloved and now, unable to restrain the ardour of her love, she breaks through the kneeling group and flings herself at his feet. In a frenzy of anxiety she grovels, implores him not to forsake her, and, clutching at his cloak, seeks to draw him to her.

The priests, scandalised beyond measure at this unseemly interruption, endeavour to seize her, but, struggling fiercely, she evades them. Again the priests stretch forth detaining hands. Torn between the conflicting emotions of love and duty, the unhappy youth knows not which way to turn. Slowly his eyes fasten on the figure kneeling before him and carried away by the fervour of the passion he had thought conquered, he casts off the priestly raiment and, raising her to her feet, clasps her in his arms. Together they strive to escape from the menacing faces that surge about them, but they are quickly captured. At a sign from the high priest the crowd disperses quietly through the door whence it came, while the young man, pinioned on each side, is carried off a close prisoner. Another signal, and chains are brought and fastened on the wrists of the struggling maiden. The priests and their attendants depart in stately procession.

The temple is empty except for the maiden shuddering

in terror and awe at the unearthly silence that surrounds her. The scene becomes darker and darker. Vainly she seeks to escape. Again her hopes are raised for glancing round she becomes aware of the low door cut in the side of the cliff. Impulsively stepping forward she opens the door and glances fearfully into the interior. Suddenly a frightful figure appears before her, an enormous lizard, which moves with slow writhing movements, swaying its horrible head at each step. More of the terrible creatures appear, to be followed by bloated giants with horrid webbed feet and hands. The reptiles form an ever-narrowing circle about her. She prostrates herself before the shrine and beseeches the clemency of the Gods.

Her prayers are not in vain for presently the sacred pool emits a bluish phosphorescent light which speedily illuminates the whole scene. From the centre of the pool the lotus rises, and, opening its petals, displays to the astonished eyes of the maiden the God and Goddess of the shrine. The first, entirely blue with tunic and crown of gold, holds in his hand a reed pipe, while the second is clothed in white and silver. The Goddess shows the unhappy maiden to her consort, whereupon the Blue God advances and, dancing round the creatures, charms them one by one into a state of senselessness.

Their mission fulfilled, the Deities prepare to depart, when there enter the priests and attendants come to view the death agonies of their victim. At the sight of the Divinities they fall prostrate before them. The Goddess bestows a blessing on the maiden and signs to them to release her. The young man is brought in and the lovers embrace. The Goddess disappears below the waters of the pool. The orange rock splits asunder revealing a flight of golden steps which the Blue God mounts and, playing on his pipe, ascends to heaven.

* *
*

The principal characters were interpreted by L. Nelidova (*The Goddess*), Karsavina (*The Young Girl*), Nijinska (*The Bayadère*), Nijinsky (*The Blue God*), Max Frohman (*The Young Man*) and Fedorov (*High Priest*).

The ballet was well received, as will be gathered from the following notice by R. Brussel :—

" The *Dieu Bleu* affords a delicious excuse for dancing, To state that its story lacks depth is at once to praise its chief quality. Its authors—I refer to those who composed the synopsis—have had no other end in view. And they have succeeded in producing a poem which owes its success to the invention or development of the plot, to the manner in which they have afforded opportunities to their collaborators—composer, painters, choreographer, or artistes. They visualised, as poets should, the atmosphere and incidents most suited to bring out the talent of a Bakst, Fokine, Karsavina, or Nijinsky, and whoever has fathomed the distinctive characters of all these artists will not fail to find the production of the *Dieu Bleu* completely appropriate to its subject.

" It is superfluous to praise Fokine. His production of *Le Dieu Bleu* is worthy of *L'Oiseau de Feu* and *Igor* ; his dances convey the illusion of spontaneity of gesture, of the liberty of the dancer, which only conceal the most rigorous order, system, and discipline. The manner in which he has arranged the scene—which has been attempted a hundred times before unsuccessfully—of the God and the monsters, is a marvel of invention, novelty, and plastic beauty[1] "

Svetlov, on the contrary, declared : " *Le Dieu Bleu* is a failure in every sense of the word—in subject, in musical composition, in setting and stage management. Its one redeeming feature is Fokine's choreography[2]."

Despite, however, the generally favourable tone of the Parisian Press, the ballet did not remain long in the repertory. Fokine's choreography revealed a careful study of the ideals of Hindu art but the ballet failed, partly on account of the poverty of the theme and still more through the music, which was neither convincing nor moving. I do not agree with Svetlov's condemnation of the setting, for in my opinion Bakst's scenery and costumes were remarkable for their originality and beauty of colour and design.

[1] *Le Figaro*, May 14th, 1912.
[2] *Op. cit.*

IV

The first of the second group of performances, which consisted of *Thamar*, with Karsavina and Bolm ; *Narcisse*, with Karsavina and Nijinsky ; *Polovtsian Dances* from *Prince Igor* ; and *Petrouchka*, with Karsavina, Nijinsky, Orlov, and Cecchetti, was given on the 20th of May.

Thamar is a ballet founded on Balakirev's symphonic poem of the same name. There is a well-known Russian legend which relates the history of a certain cruel Thamar, Queen of Georgia, who in the twelfth century lived with her court in a lonely castle built on the precipitous heights of the Dariel Gorge, through which pour the stormy waters of the Terek. It was her wont, under the guise of hospitality, to entice into her castle the travellers who passed by that deserted road. Then, having enchanted them by her beauty, she would kill them and cause their bodies to be hurled over the mountain side. With this theme in his mind Lermontov wrote his poem " Thamar." In turn, under the influence of the poem, Balakirev composed his symphony, so full of colour and analogy that it is not difficult to trace the story of the legend during a performance of the work. The thought of uniting both music and poem in a ballet originated with Bakst, who also designed the scenery and costumes.

* *
*

The scene shows a large, rectangular room with a high roof which slopes to an acute angle. The walls are of brick, shaded from rose to deep violet. Around the base of the walls, for about the height of a man, runs a broad crimson tapestry, decorated with large circles rimmed with a blue and white chequer. At the back, to the left, is a heavily-studded green door, at the side of which is an ikon set in a tryptych. To the right is a large turret window, half-covered by a heavy curtain, which reveals a glimpse of snow-clad mountains. The last rays of a pale sunset lighten the green-carpeted floor. From the centre of the roof hangs a crude candelabrum set with candles which smoke and flicker under the gales that sweep about the castle. The room is strewn with rich carpets and costly skins, but, despite the splendour of the appointments, there is an atmosphere of gloom and unrest.

Near the window is a table loaded with flagons. Beside this stands a couch upon which reclines Thamar, Queen of Georgia. She is attired in a light crimson caftan while her hair is gathered into two long plaits threaded with a string of pearls.

To the left of the room, in a recess, a band of musicians is seated. Women and guards are grouped about the walls. Some converse in low tones, others are silent and impassive. Thamar turns uneasily on her couch. An attendant inclines her head as if straining at a sound. She darts forward on tip-toe, bends over the queen and whispers in her ear. Thamar languidly raises herself on one elbow and peers intently through the darkening window. Then she gropes among her cushions and withdraws a scarf. With a jerk of her wrist it waves in the air—once, twice, and thrice. A pause. The signal has been observed and answered.

A ripple of expectation passes over the waiting men and women. The queen rises and steps to the floor. With an imperative gesture she summons three of her guards who fling long, black cloaks over their shoulders and pass out to welcome the guest. The music, till now almost unnoticed, becomes more insistent, even ominous, as the guards return accompanied by a tall stranger, cloaked from head to foot, his face half-hidden by a scarf drawn tight about his throat and chin.

Thamar gazes at him with intensity as if in endeavour to divine his features. Impatient, she flings back the scarf to reveal a handsome youth. They look steadfastly at each other, then he extends his arms as if to embrace her, but she eludes his grasp and signs to the guards to relieve him of his cloak. She offers him wine which he drinks. The traveller bends over her, but the women close about him and usher him from the chamber.

The queen remains standing, deep in thought. She summons her warriors to dance. In single file the guards sweep forward in a semi-circle. With a jerk of their hands they pluck daggers from their sheaths and whirl their arms in a circular movement, so that the bright steel describes a series of glittering arcs. They dance with frenzied bounds, with fierce stamps of the feet; the measure becomes wilder and wilder. The music throbs and pulsates with a maddening rhythm. Soon they lose all restraint. The daggers are raised in the air to be hurled viciously into the floor. But scarcely have they ceased quivering when they are wrenched from their sockets, to be hurled down again. The music swells in an ever-increasing volume of sound. Thamar, a little apart, surveys the scene with outward sign of increasing passion. Unable to restrain her impatience, she imperiously stamps her foot.

The door opens and the stranger enters, clad in a splendid caftan. He is surrounded by a group of women who bear large tambourines. They wind about the room with languorous movements the while they strike their tambourines. The stranger quickly espies the queen and strives to approach her, but she affects to ignore him. She retreats through her waiting women and makes her way to the couch, with her lover following hard at her heels. He seeks to win her favour with a dance. He springs into the air, jerks his head to and fro, and curves his legs under him so that, with every leap, his body is arched like a strung bow. He bounds higher and higher, his feet stamp, twist, and turn, faster and faster, to the frenzied throbbing of the tambourines. The queen marks with satisfaction his feverish looks, his savage movements. She joins in the dance and their lips meet in a passionate kiss. Then she twists from his grasp and runs through the green door. He follows in pursuit.

Their disappearance is an excuse for the resumption of the mad dance of a short while since. The eye can scarce support the turmoil of nodding hats, wind-blown garments, gleaming daggers—the vivid purples, greens, and reds of the costumes intermingled in one scintillating, revolving mass. The floor echoes to the pulsating rhythm of the measured stamp of heel and toe. At last, overcome with exhaustion, the dancers cease and lean against the walls to rest their weary, aching limbs.

Again the youth re-enters. He staggers backward into the room as if his legs were incapable of supporting his frame. Now Thamar appears, her eyes lowered, her nostrils dilated, her features set in a grim and sinister mask. She comes to him, leans over his face with a seductive smile, then throws an arm about his neck and drags him to and fro. Meanwhile, two attendants pull back a cunningly-devised panel set in the wall, through which, sparkling in the pearl-grey light of dawn, can be seen the swiftly-falling waters of the Terek. Stealthily she unsheathes the dagger at her girdle. She draws him closer, kisses his eyes and, with a quick movement of her arm, stabs him to the heart. The wretched youth struggles from her embrace, totters from side, to side and falls backward through the panel. The attendants close the door.

The queen steps towards her couch and summons her women who loosen her hair and divest her of her outer garments. She flings herself upon the couch and closes her eyes. Again a woman inclines her head in an attitude of listening. She lightly touches the slumbering queen and whispers in her ear. Thamar half-rises and gazes through the turret window. She fumbles among her cushions and withdraws the scarf. Again it writhes in the air—once, twice, thrice. . . .

* *
*

Thamar is a fine example of a dramatic ballet. Fokine had visited the Caucasus in his youth, and he drew on these memories for his inspiration for the dances, which are extraordinarily fierce and thrilling. He has no equal in the arrangement of dances which require to be imbued with a mad frenzy. The wonderful manner in which he combines movement with rhythm, the endless combinations of colour which he evolves from the varied order and movement of the costumes, so excite the spectator that it requires the greatest effort for him to observe the social conventions which demand that he shall remain quietly seated in his place. The mimed scenes are most impressive

94

and it is remarkable how the queen, though never rendered obtrusive, is made to dominate the whole like some evil spirit drawn by Vrubel. From the moment the curtain rises, the action, swift and tense, keeps the spectator enthralled to the very end.

"Fokine," wrote a critic, "is the arranger of the dances in *Thamar* and never except in *Schéhérazade* have we witnessed a greater power of invention. In order to render justice to this great artist we ought to enumerate the figures he has created in *Thamar*, their intense variety and character, the manner in which they blend, the way in which they begin, develop, and reach their climax, then die down only to burst forth anew with even greater frenzy. Never has the choregraphic art been carried so near perfection and displayed so much originality[1]."

v

The first of the third series of performances, given on the 29th of May, consisted of *Le Spectre de la Rose*, *Le Dieu Bleu*, *L'Oiseau de Feu*, and a new ballet, *L'Après-Midi d'un Faune*. Since this was arranged by Vaslav Nijinsky it does not come within the scope of this volume. It would seem, however, that Nijinsky's desire to achieve fame as a choregrapher, an ambition which received every encouragement from Diaghilev, had the inevitable consequences of engendering friction in the company.

The first of the fourth and last group of performances, which was announced for the 5th of June, consisted of *Daphnis et Chloé*, *Schéhérazade*, and *Thamar*. Now the production of *Daphnis*, which had been assigned to Fokine, did not proceed smoothly. The time accorded for rehearsals was insufficient. Again, the nymphs in *L'Après-Midi d'un Faune* were given new dresses and beautiful gold wigs with flowing, crinkled hair in the Grecian style; but the *corps de ballet* in *Daphnis* had to dress their hair as best they could, while the costumes were not new, but picked out from previous ballets, principally *Narcisse*. As a consequence of the hindrances and disputes that arose, the

[1] *Le Figaro*, May 22nd, 1912.

95

ballet was not ready by the 5th, and Diaghilev wished Fokine to cancel the production, pointing out that the final dance, which occupied twenty pages of music, had not even been begun. Fokine replied that he would finish the ballet at all costs.

He detailed various movements to a number of small groups which then broke up so that the members filled the stage; they then turned and the ballet was completed with one short but impressive dance by the entire company. All this was accomplished in one rehearsal. This method of quickly producing a big dance, which was arranged to a very difficult rhythm—5–8, most unusual in ballet music—was adopted by Fokine in order to complete the ballet quickly, but, despite the circumstances under which it was composed, he has since seen no reason to change it.

Daphnis et Chloé was finally given on the 8th of June, but now, to add to Fokine's trials, it was announced that the ballet would be the first on the programme, and the performance given half-an-hour earlier than usual, which meant that the ballet would be given under unfavourable conditions. Fokine was very angered by this announcement and immediately sought the director, with whom he had a violent altercation; as a result the ballet was given in the middle of the evening's performance, although it was placed first in the printed programme.

The *scenario* of *Daphnis et Chloé* is the same as that originally written by Fokine in 1904, which it will be remembered was in two acts. The present ballet consisted of the first act only, which falls into three scenes. The second act was never finished, nor has the music been written for it. The scenery was designed by Leon Bakst.

The principal characters were interpreted by Karsavina (*Chloé*), M. Frohman (*Lisinion*), Nijinsky (*Daphnis*), Bolm (*Darkon*), and Cecchetti (*Lammon*).

* *
*

The first scene represents a grove sacred to Pan and his Nymphs. The background is formed by a group of cypresses bounded by large boulders; in the distance can be seen rising fields dotted with scattered bushes. To the right and left of the foreground are similar groups of cypresses, that on the left being flanked by a rocky eminence upon which stand out in sharp relief the sculptured forms of three nymphs, marking the rough altar erected to the glory of the God Pan.

Soon there arrives a procession of graceful maidens bearing on their heads baskets and oval jars which contain offerings for the altar—wine pressed from the choicest grapes, fruit plucked from the finest orchards, flowers culled from the fairest fields. Slowly, with infinite variety of pose and gesture, the maidens wind about the altar. Now they are joined by young men who also take part in these solemn measures.

The rites ended, the worshippers break up into little groups. Among the throng can be seen the handsome Daphnis and the fair Chloë, lovers from their tenderest years. Daphnis casts many spells over the hearts of the young girls present. Soon, ever willing to please, he joins them in a dance which arouses Chloë's jealousy. In revenge, she wanders among the young men and becomes in consequence the object of the attentions of Darkon, a boorish herdsman whose sole claim to admiration lies in his immense physical strength.

He becomes bolder and attempts to snatch a kiss, which inclination is prevented by the timely intervention of Daphnis. It is clear that the rivals will soon fall to blows, but the shepherds will have none of it and bid them match their prowess in a dance. Darkon, already convinced of his superiority, executes a clumsy dance with much stamping of feet, shaking of head, and wild flinging of his arms. The onlookers burst into laughter, and Darkon, seeing that his efforts excite only derision, retires in scornful humiliation. Then it is the turn of Daphnis who, taking in his hand a white wand, performs a graceful dance which is received with applause. Chloë, her anger past, bestows on him a kiss. Now all leave the grove save Daphnis who, spent with the exertion of the dance, composes himself on the ground to rest. No sooner is his head pillowed on the turf than evil befalls him in the guise of the temptress Lisinion. She unveils and with langourous dance seeks to captivate him, but Daphnis angrily repulses her and bids her begone. She departs in dismay.

Suddenly there is heard the noise of running feet, the clash of warlike weapons, the hoarse cries of lawless men, mingled with the pitiful shrieks of women who, fleeing in terror, seek to escape from the merciless pirates who have just landed in quest of plunder. The voices come nearer, and Chloë, gasping for breath, seeks sanctuary in the sacred grove. But the pirates have no scruples and one of their number seizes Chloë, throws her over his shoulder, and disappears.

All has passed in an instant and before Daphnis, stupified by the clamour, can run to her aid, the grove is empty and in place of Chloë there remains only her torn scarf trodden deep into the earth. Distraught, he curses the gods and falls in a swoon.

The shadows fall and dusk deepens into night. A mysterious light illumines the altar and out of the darkness appear the three Nymphs who with reverent gesture and solemn dance invoke the aid of Pan.

*

The second scene shows the pirates' camp, a vast clearing, almost surmounted by great, orange-brown cliffs. Between two of these can be seen a glimpse of the Ægean Sea where their ship rides at anchor. Overhead a blue sky glows across which float sun-streaked masses of cloud as if to imitate the motion of the ship below.

Again that awful tumult falls on the ears and the pirates arrive, laden with booty and dragging in their midst the trembling Chloë. They call for a dance, and, shouting with drunken glee, seize their bows and spears and bound and leap in a circle. They quarrel and wrestle among themselves, howling and struggling like a pack of dogs. But at a signal from their chief they cease their dangerous play and all is quiet. With a grin he beckons to Chloë, but unwilling, she has to be half-carried, half-dragged to his presence. She begs for pity but the chief only grins the more, and stretching out his arm pulls her on to his knee.

Suddenly a strange shadow falls over the cliffs, at the sight of which the pirates tremble with superstitious fear. The shadow comes nearer and the pirates, relinquishing their captive, flee in terror. Chloë falls on her knees and offers up a prayer of thanksgiving.

*

The third and last scene returns to the sacred grove. Here Daphnis, awakened from his trance, ponders deeply on the loss of his beloved. But how can he avail against a score of fierce pirates ! He is about to leave when Chloë runs to his arms. They embrace, their friends return, and there are mutual congratulations. Now together, hand in hand, the happy couple are betrothed before the altar consecrated to Pan, and the scene ends with a joyful dance in celebration.

**
*

During the performance of *Daphnis et Chloé* there was another drama being enacted behind the scenes. The artistes had learned of the dispute between Diaghilev and Fokine, which ended in the latter's resignation, and the company divided into two parties. Those who wished to display their gratitude to Fokine for the success they had gained in dancing in his ballets, prepared a large bouquet of flowers contained in a beautiful vase, which they desired to offer him on the stage. But this Nijinsky would not permit, although at the conclusion of the ballet they took their calls together : Nijinsky in his costume as Daphnis, Fokine in evening dress.

Fokine went home sad at heart, feeling that he had ended his activities in a company which he honestly considered to be his own creation. But when he arrived at his hotel he found the group of artistes there waiting with the flowers and vase which they had not been able to present to him in public. This pathetic scene of farewell took place at the Hôtel des Deux Mondes.

The reception of *Daphnis et Chloé* by the public was most enthusiastic, the critics were no less cordial. Robert Brussel, in the notice he contributed to the *Figaro*[1] the following day, has summed up the ballet so well that it will be sufficient to reproduce his words :—

" It must be regretted that *Daphnis et Chloé* appeared so late in the programme of the Russian Ballet, nor is it less to be regretted that it can only be given twice. It is the work of a French composer, which fact makes it of particular interest to us, and furthermore it is the most perfect and poetical work which we owe to the artistic enterprise of M. Serge de Diaghilev.

" I do not know whether *Daphnis et Chloé* is what is termed a ' manifestation,' that is to say, whether it reverses present opinion, or reveals a depth of humanity hitherto unknown. I only know that it is, or at least I believe it to be, a marvellously gifted and tender work full of suggestion ; it presents the most agreeable scenes and incidents which evoke deep feeling, for the ballet is the work of a poet and an artist. This gives the whole an exceptional character, rather than any surprising detail, which doubtless would not fail to arouse ecstasy. Thus its title of ' *symphonie chorégraphique* ' need not astonish us nor cause us to misinterpret its purpose. *Daphnis et Chloé* is a ballet and in according it this title I have no wish to offend its authors or lessen their merit. To renew a form which has served as a model, to infuse new life into material about to perish, is a more difficult, a more useful, work, than to aspire to the exceptional with mediocre means and to create a fashion rather than solve an artistic difficulty.

" *Daphnis et Chloé* then is a genuine work of art which, in a setting enriched by the most noble tradition, concedes nothing or almost nothing to present fashion, does not court easy success, and, being neither reactionary nor a false prophecy of the future, is in the best taste of the present day as works should be which aspire to influence profoundly their epoch.

[1] June 9th, 1912.

" Michel Fokine, at once author and producer, has afforded in *Daphnis et Chloé*, a new proof of his extraordinary talent. He has perhaps imagined more astonishing pictures, but he has never evoked one more delicate or more expressive. The dances he has arranged for Daphnis, Chloë, and the grotesque Darkon are wonderfully varied ; that of Daphnis is light, that of Chloë tender or mournful, that of Darkon clumsy, and all this is expressed in the most diverse, appropriate, and pathetic manner."

CHAPTER TEN

PRODUCTION OF " LES PRÉLUDES," " THE SEVEN DAUGHTERS
OF THE MOUNTAIN KING," " LA LÉGENDE DE JOSEPH,"
AND " LE COQ D'OR "

I

AFTER the break with Diaghilev Fokine was very de-
pressed, and so discouraged at being absent from the
company which he had trained, that for some time he could
not work. Then, early in 1913, he received an invitation
from Madame Anna Pavlova to come to Berlin, where
she then was, to produce some ballets. He accepted and
when asked to offer a theme suggested that a ballet might
be based on Rimsky-Korsakov's opera, *Le Coq d'Or*. But
she considered this to be too political in substance and,
further, that it would be inexpedient to present a burlesque
portrait of a Tsar. Hence, after further consultation,
Fokine devised two other ballets, *Les Préludes and The
Seven Daughters of the Mountain King*.

The first ballet was inspired by the paintings of Botticelli
and arranged to Liszt's *Les Préludes* which, suggested to
the composer by Larmartine's *Méditations Poétiques*, was
conceived at Marseille in 1845 and completed at Weimar
in 1850. It has no theme but is symbolical of man's
eternal struggle between life and death. The scenery,
designed by B. Anisfeld, was rather cubist in treatment.
The principal parts were taken by Pavlova and Novikov.
Both Nikisch and Strauss were present at the ballet's first performance and complimented the choreographer on his success.

The second ballet, produced at the same period, was
based on Lermontov's poem, *The Three Palms*. The
music was by Spendiarov ; the theme was composed after
the poem by Fokine and Anisfeld, the designer of the
scenery and costumes.

II

This is the story of the ballet. The Seven Daughters of
the King of the Black Mountains are dissatisfied with their

SETTING BY BORIS ANISFELD FOR " LES PRÉLUDES "

SCENE FROM " LA LÉGENDE DE JOSEPH "

master, for they lead a dreary existence. Being winged girls they are unacquainted with human passions and are jealous of mankind. They resemble caged birds. The king overhears their complaints and becomes angry. Now a caravan draws near and a handsome youth, attended by slaves bearing costly goods, enters the palace where no man has set foot before. The maidens wait on the welcome guests and the men sleep in their arms.

Presently, the angry voice of the master is heard. Fire bursts from the ground, consumes the girls' wings, symbol of divine purity, and burns their bodies. When dawn breaks the members of the caravan depart, indifferent to the sudden disappearance of their hostesses. One girl alone remains in the palace. She is the sister who has not sinned and who did not complain. Overcome with sadness at the fate of her sisters she pines away. All is quiet save for the plashing of the fountain in the deserted palace. She goes to the spring which falls lower and lower and dries up. The girl is dead.

*
* *

After producing these two ballets Fokine returned to St. Petersburg. In the meantime many untoward events had taken place in the Diaghilev organisation. Nijinsky's third ballet, *Le Sacre de Printemps*, which had required 120 rehearsals, was performed six times only, and later in the year, while the company was on tour in South America, he married and severed his association with Diaghilev, being determined to start on his own account.

III

Now Diaghilev came to Fokine and begged him to return and save the company. At first he refused to meet or even correspond with him. Some days later the critic Svetlov, who lived in the same house as Fokine, on the Ekaterininsky Canal, telephoned to him that Diaghilev was in his flat. Would not Fokine receive him? After some moments of irresolution he agreed, and a little later Diaghilev entered his room. It was a most embarrassing moment. The impresario stated that the troupe was in danger as it no longer possessed a choregrapher, and he begged Fokine to resume his former position. At first he refused, but the thought that his ballets were perhaps being given incorrectly, and the possibility that he might create better ones, induced him to waver. Further meetings took place as a result of which he agreed to revive the old ballets and produce seven new ones.

The result of Fokine's return to the company was seen in the programme given at the following Paris season (May to June, 1914) at the Opera, when the repertory announced included four new productions, a revival of *Papillons* (previously given only in St. Petersburg), *La Légende de Joseph, Midas,* and the opera *Le Coq d'Or.*

IV

The first two were given on the 14th of May. *La Légende de Joseph* was written by Hugo von Hoffmansthal and Count Harry Kessler. This piece was not so much a ballet as a wordless play in the manner of *Sumurun.* It contained many dances, but these were more in the manner of embroidery than a necessary adjunct to the plot. Though founded on the ancient legend which remains in its entirety, the action is transferred to Venice, of the sixteenth century. The costumes by Bakst were all in the manner of Paolo Veronese with the exception of those worn by Joseph and the dealers, which were Oriental dresses of the same period. The music was composed by Richard Strauss.

* *
*

The scene, designed by J. M. Sert, represents a great pillared hall. The walls, a little higher than a tall man, are built of rectangular bricks, seemingly of solid gold. Along the top of the wall runs a loggia composed of massive, convoluted columns, which scintillate with a metallic green lustre like the wing-case of a scarabeus. Through these can be seen a deep blue sky, here and there obstructed by the tops of tall palms. At the left is an arched doorway, to the right is a flight of steps leading to the loggia.

104

At the back, against the wall, runs a long table, set on a raised platform and flanked on the left by a short table raised on three broad steps. Both are covered with white cloths on which gleam gold beakers and crystal flagons of wine, and gold platters piled high with fruit and viands. Behind the long table sit the guests, ladies in gorgeous brocades, nobles in costly doublets and slashed trunks.

At the raised table Potiphar is seated, an imposing figure in velvet and ermine. Beside him is his wife, dressed in a robe of red brocade, heavy with gold embroidery. Grouped about the walls stand Potiphar's bodyguard, tall negroes in black and yellow, their breasts protected with gold corslets. For arms they bear gold halberds and long whips with short handles.

The scene presents a marvellous spectacle of the wealth and might of Potiphar. Bored to the last degree, he lazily sips from a tall beaker that stands in front of him. Satiated with all that life can offer, it is certain that for him there remains no pleasure untasted, no sensation unrealised. His is indeed a world " in which the air seems charged with gold dust." A sheik advances and begs permission to display his wares. In quick succession he disposes of a bowl filled with precious stones, a carpet of wondrous colours, and a pair of greyhounds.

At a gesture from Potiphar slaves advance and lay the gifts at his wife's feet. Another slave comes to the sheik carrying scales and bags of gold. For a moment little is heard but the trickle of the gold dust in the pan as the sheik receives the amount of Potiphar's purchases. He bows low and prepares to depart, but at a signal from Potiphar remains. Now enters a band of women, some veiled, some unveiled. Together they perform a slow, languid dance swaying gently from the hips. Suddenly a single dancer detaches herself from the group and dances alone. At the conclusion she advances to Potiphar's wife, but with an impatient gesture is dismissed. The dancers file out slowly while along the loggia passes a band of men, nude except for a short skirt about their loins, who descend into the hall.

They are boxers who after massaging their muscles commence to give an exhibition of their art. Slowly, walking with stealthy, cat-like tread, they move around each other in a circle, seeking to take their opponent at a disadvantage. At first the dance is a display and nothing more, but gradually their brutish instincts come to the fore and they begin to fight in real earnest, intent only on the killing of their opponent. But at a sign from Potiphar the men-at-arms separate them with lashes from their long whips. The boxers cower like beaten dogs and flee through the arched doorway.

Potiphar nods to the sheik who makes a sign in the direction of the loggia. Enter two negro slaves bearing a hammock on their shoulders. Behind them follow a group of shepherd boys, some with cymbals in their hands, others with flutes. The hammock is lowered to the ground. It contains a sleeping boy. The sheik awakens him and assists him to his feet. It is Joseph. He stands there clad only in a short white goat-skin, his eyes open to their fullest extent at the splendour that surrounds him.

His companions sit on the ground and play simple airs, to which he dances round and round. At first, the measure is clumsily performed and his whole attitude expresses innocence and freedom. Gradually he becomes hypnotised by the circular movement and his actions become more pleasing, more refined, as if he had received divine inspiration. Again the dance changes, expressive of the supreme joy of spiritual comfort; then it ceases and he assumes the simple demeanour of a shepherd boy.

During his dance the guests whisper one to another in endeavour to determine what lies behind his rude exterior. For the first time Potiphar's wife relaxes her haughty mien and shows deep interest in Joseph's dances. Her quivering lips and gleaming eyes betoken her agitation. Potiphar makes a sign; he will buy this wonderful youth. Again a slave goes to the sheik and the trickle of gold dust in the scale pan is heard once more.

Potiphar's wife rises to her feet and, drawing the bowl of precious stones toward her, takes a jewelled collaret

from it.   A slave leads Joseph to the daïs which he slowly
mounts.   As he approaches she rests her left hand on his
neck and with the other clasps on the collaret.   Then, as if
ashamed of her weakness, she turns from him.   Potiphar
frowns suspiciously at his wife, rises, and signs for the
feast to end.

They descend from the daïs and mount the steps leading
to the loggia, behind them follows the train of guests.
The sheik and his slaves bow low and pass through the
arched doorway.   Joseph remains standing in a respectful
attitude.

*

The scene remains unchanged except that now it is dark.
In the centre of the wall at the back is a recess, dimly lit,
containing a low couch.   Joseph kneels beside it in prayer,
then lies on the couch and falls asleep.

A light flickers at the far end of the loggia and a woman
in white, carrying a small lamp, approaches and descends
into the hall.   She goes to Joseph's couch and, raising
the lamp so that its rays fall on his features, contemplates
them in ecstasy.   She touches his cheek and as if aghast at
her temerity extinguishes the lamp.

Joseph awakes and, seeing in the woman before him the
vision of his dreams, believes her to be an angel.   He
stretches out his hand towards her.   She falls on her knees
and loosening her hair covers her face.   Then she bends
down and kisses him.   At this Joseph leaps up and flees
into the centre of the hall, where he cowers, covering
himself with his cloak.   She follows and tries to raise him
to his feet.   For an instant he remains in prayer, then
draws himself up, extends a hand as if to ward off a blow,
and looks at her in horror.   She clutches at his cloak but
he holds it firm.   Then with a quick movement he steps
to one side and casts it from him, gazing at her in contempt.
She falls to her knees and seems to implore pardon, but
he remains unmoved.   Overcome with rage, she leaps to
her feet and tries to strangle him.   They struggle, then she
is forced slowly to her knees.

Again a light appears at the far end of the loggia, and

attendants, alarmed at the noise, run down the steps into the hall. Potiphar's wife rises and with a regal gesture commands them to arrest Joseph. He who disdained pleasure may now taste torture. There is an ominous silence, then with measured tread Potiphar enters with his men-at-arms. They advance and chain Joseph hand and foot.

Potiphar turns to his wife who with half-closed eyes offers him her lips to kiss. He caresses her to soothe her agitation. Then she points dramatically at Joseph. At this Potiphar stamps his foot with fury. Now several executioners enter bearing in their midst a gigantic brazier. They busy themselves about the brazier reviving the dying embers with the bellows. The embers glow and burst into flame. The men stir them about and begin to heat pointed irons. Joseph remains calm, his face uplifted. Suddenly a radiant light shines and across the loggia and down the steps walks a glittering angel. He advances, touches Joseph on the shoulder, and his chains fall from him ; then the angel takes the youth by the hand and leads him up the steps.

The frightened attendants seem rooted to the ground. Then some fall prostrate, others shield their eyes, fearful lest a ray from the glorious being should strike them dead. Potiphar's wife, astonished at the interruption, becomes terrified, then stretches out her arms as if seeking to follow Joseph and the angel. But suddenly her face becomes drawn, her teeth clench, and clutching at the rope of pearls about her neck, she draws it tighter and tighter, strangling herself. A last gasp and she falls dead.

* *
*

The principal parts were taken as follows : Maria Kusnetzova (*Potiphar's wife*), Vera Fokina (*the Shulamite woman*), Alexis Bulgakov (*Potiphar*), and Leonide Massine (*Joseph*).

Some indication of the manner in which this ballet was received may be gathered from this notice of the first performance which appeared in *Le Figaro* : " Yesterday its success was a complete triumph. It was affirmed by

lengthy ovations and repeated calls before the curtain.
The pomp and magnificence of the spectacle, the opulent
and singular taste which distinguishes the whole production,
reflects the greatest honour on M. Michel Fokine, the
producer of this incomparable spectacle."

V

The first performance of *Le Coq d'Or* took place on the
21st of May. When this production had been decided on,
Fokine was anxious that it should be staged in as modern
a manner as possible. Benois suggested that Nathalie
Gontcharova would be an excellent artist to design the
costumes and scenery, but Fokine decided to reserve his
decision. Finally, in company with Benois and Diaghilev,
he went to the artist's home in Moscow. They arrived
at night-time and saw specimens of her work by candle-
light, which gave additional strength to her impressive,
grotesque, and brilliantly-coloured drawings. Fokine felt
Gontcharova's work to be very suited to the proposed
ballet and the artist was given the commission to design
the necessary scenery and costumes.

Le Coq d'Or is an opera-ballet composed by Rimsky-
Korsakov to a libretto by V. Bielsky, based on the
well-known poem by Pushkin. It possesses not only a
legendary character but also an undercurrent of pointed
satire, which contributes considerably to its remarkable
originality.

The Fokine production was conceived in a manner then
probably unique, for the cast was divided into two parts,
operatic and choreographic, that is to say, while one character acted and danced, the words spoken by this character
were sung by his or her counterpart in the vocal cast,
producing a most unusual effect.

* *
*

Before the curtain rises there is a short prologue, in
which an old astrologer, in characteristic conical hat and
black gown, informs the audience that the piece about to
be presented, though a fairy tale, is not without its moral.

109

Barely has he departed when the curtain rises to unfold
a scene which, for wealth of colour, fantasy, and imagination, it would be difficult to surpass. To right and left of
the stage, grouped in tiers like an oratorio choir, are male
and female singers, dressed in crimson. These choirs
remain seated throughout the play. In regard to the
scene proper, the background is formed by a low, yellow
wall, upon which are depicted curious animals in a fighting
attitude, while along its base grow miniature bushes of a
vivid green. In the centre of the wall is a gate, let into a
lofty arch, bounded on each side by a high pointed tower,
lavishly decorated with a broad floral design in reddish
brown. Above the wall rise the varied towers and spires
of a town.

The left wing is formed by enormous brown houses, and
a tall green tree, bearing white blossoms of monstrous size,
in appearance not unlike a giant narcissus ; to the right
are similar houses and another giant tree, deep brown in
hue, with fronds like those of a palm tree, from which
depend green, rose, and yellow flowers. At the left centre
stands a four-poster bed of fantastic design, which, like the
floor, is of reddish-brown.

The aged King Dodon with his sons and advisers are
taking council together as to the best means of defending
the kingdom against a threatening neighbour. After much
foolish advice has been proffered and discussed, the company, unable to find a satisfactory solution to the problem,
fall to quarrelling among themselves, when suddenly the
Astrologer of the prologue appears. He offers the King
the gift of a magic golden cockerel which will always give
warning of the presence of danger.

At first the King refuses to believe him, until the bird
having been brought in, commences by telling the King
to reign at his ease, at which he is so delighted that he
promises the Astrologer what he will. The latter, satisfied
with such munificence, departs to ponder over the form his
reward shall take, while the King, relieved of responsibility,
intimates a desire to slumber and is put to bed. The court,
unable to think of anything better to do, go to sleep

likewise.   Meanwhile, the ladies-in-waiting, grotesquely attired, dance round the King's bed, waving handkerchiefs as they go, to drive away the flies.

All at once the cock crows : " Danger, beware ! "   The King awakes with a start, despatches the unwilling princes in charge of a select body of troops to deal with the menace, and resumes his sleep.   There is much humour in the departure of the warriors.   All are bearded, ferocious of expression, and armed to the teeth.   They march off with slow jerky movements like those of a clockwork toy.

Again the cock crows : " Danger ! " and this time the King, having no one else to send, is forced to undertake the business himself.   This episode is no less amusing in the actions of the portly monarch who grumblingly tries to mount a huge wooden horse.   First he drops his sword, then his shield, until at last, after a period of utter exasperation, he succeeds in mounting his charger, to the relief of all concerned, and, accompanied by the remainder of the army, sets forth to defend his country, amid the acclamations of the court.

*

The second act transports the action to the frontier, a scene in sharp contrast to the first, for all is black, dismal, and veiled in mist.   Here Dodon and his followers wander over what has evidently been the field of battle.   Corpses are piled thickly and in the centre lie the bodies of his two sons, a sword standing upright in each.   At this miserable sight the doddering old man is reduced to tears, when suddenly the mist clears and a large green tent, seemingly risen from the ground, is revealed to the astonished onlookers.

With considerable apprehension the soldiers prepare for battle, but the curtains are softly drawn back and from the interior emerges the beautiful Queen of Shemâkhan, so fascinating a vision that the King thinks of nothing but other kinds of conquests.   Now a band of women come from the tent and seating themselves on the ground begin the prelude to a dance.   The Queen dances slowly with languorous movements, swaying to the rhythm of the music, her lips parted in a mocking smile.

III

The King, hopelessly infatuated with such beauty and scarcely knowing whether he is on his head or his heels, soon surrenders, while the visitor further strengthens her position by inducing him to dance too. In high humour he assents, but only succeeds in making himself a lamentable and ridiculous spectacle, at the sight of which even his hardened court give way to laughter. At last, breathless and exhausted, he sinks to the ground. At his request the Queen consents to be his bride and accompanied by the court and army they set out for the capital.

*

The third and final scene depicts the exterior of the palace of the first act. There is seen the fronts of two huge palaces, with turrets and steeples protruding at all manner of queer places. Except for the shaded pink bricks composing the buildings, the whole is carried out again in reddish-brown, green, and yellow. The assembled populace await the return of their beloved monarch and his bride.

Soon the procession enters, headed by an advance guard of warriors, followed by the King and Queen seated in an extraordinary chariot, heavily gilt and guarded by a grotesque band of slaves, waiting women, and further warriors. The King, despite his anxious and careworn appearance, gazes with loving tenderness at his consort, while she looks the picture of utter boredom.

A clap of thunder resounds and again the Astrologer enters. Dodon receives him with great goodwill and expresses his willingness to bestow the promised reward for the present of the golden cockerel, whereupon the Astrologer demands the Queen of Shemâkhan. At this the King's anger passes all bounds and, in a rage, he strikes him on the head with his sceptre.

The Queen laughs cynically at this untoward incident, but Dodon, fearful of his deed, begins to bemoan the consequences. He begs sympathy from his bride, but now, no longer simulating affection, she reproaches him. Suddenly the golden cockerel flies to the King and striking him down with a blow of its beak lays him dead. Again is heard a clap of thunder followed by a short period of darkness. When all is light both bird and Queen have disappeared, and the curtain falls on the sorrowing populace.

Again the Astrologer appears before the curtain and informs the audience that, with the exception of himself and the Queen, there were no real people in the piece, the rest was but a dream.

* *
*

The principal characters were interpreted thus : T. Karsavina (*Queen of Shemâkhan*), Mme. Jezierska (*Amelfa*), A. Bulgakov (*King Dodon*), E. Cecchetti (*Astrologer*), Kovalski (*General Polkan*), S. Grigoriev (*Guidone*), and M. Frohman (*Afrone*).

Le Coq d'Or was received with extraordinary applause. A critic, writing of Fokine, declared : " The dispositions invented by him for *Le Coq d'Or*, the *divertissements*, marches, and processions, are all marked by an unusual sense of the burlesque or sumptuous fantasy which one cannot but admire."

VI

Midas was a ballet in the Greek manner. The scenery and costumes were designed by M. Dobuzhinsky, the music was the second of Maximilien Steinberg's " Metamorphoses," which is arranged in three movements.

The theme, by Leon Bakst, deals with the contest in minstrelsy between Pan and Apollo. The contest is held at the foot of Mount Tomlus, and the mountain and forest divinities are to judge. Pan plays his pipes and Apollo his lyre. The presiding deity pronounces in favour of Apollo, which verdict is acclaimed by all, save Midas. He prefers Pan and declares the award partial. Thereupon Apollo, much to the delight of the onlookers, decorates Midas with a pair of ass's ears in token of his stupidity.

* *
*

The principal characters were taken as follows : T. Karsavina (*Oreade*), Adolph Bolm (*Midas*), M. Frohman (*Apollo*), and B. Romanov (*Pan*).

Although the ballet contained some charming dances for Karsavina as Oreade, the ballet as a whole was not very entertaining and failed to achieve success.

VII

At the close of the London season, at which the Diaghilev Company made their usual appearance, Fokine went to Spain where he remained some three months, visiting Madrid, Seville, Malaga, and Granada. He studied the national dances everywhere, in the mountains, from gypsies, from dancers, and in the villages.

He saw some excellent dancers in Malaga where he met an old woman who taught peasant dances, of which she knew over seventy. She had a small room in which her pupils all played the castanets and danced in turn. She went to Fokine's hotel with a guitarist, and he tried to write down the airs, but although she knew them by heart she was quite unacquainted with musical notation and inquired of Fokine what strange language he was writing.

I

THE year 1915 was marked by the production of three new ballets by Fokine, all of widely different character, given in the cause of charity at the Maryinsky Theatre on the 28th of November. The proceeds were devoted to the opening of a home for poor children who had lost their fathers in the War. These ballets were *Francesca da Rimini*, *Eros*, and *Stenka Razin*.

The theme of the first was taken by Fokine from Dante's *Divina Comedia* and arranged to Tchaikovsky's " Fantasia for Orchestra : Francesca da Rimini." The scenery was contrived from that of old operas and ballets. The manner of production was quite new. The action was from time to time transferred to different parts of the stage and lighted accordingly in sections, so that the setting for the succeeding episodes could be prepared in readiness in that portion of the stage that was temporarily in darkness.

It is of interest to note that *Francesca da Rimini* was given after only one rehearsal on the stage, when the costumes were tried on, the changes of scenery practised, the lighting-plot worked out, several " aerial flights " tested, and the ballet given with the orchestra—*all in one rehearsal.* Moreover on this same occasion Fokine rehearsed the other two ballets which composed the programme—*Eros* and *Stenka Razin* ; the last-named also contained difficulties on account of the large ship and numerous properties that figure in the ballet.

II

Francesca da Rimini, which was based on Canto V of the *Inferno*, begins in the same manner in the second circle of Hell, with a flight of carnal sinners who are tossed about ceaselessly by furious winds. Dante and Virgil are seen looking down on them from a high rock. Two lovers approach Dante and in response to his request tell him the sad story of their love. The story is then treated in the manner of a kinematographic " flash-back," and shown in a series of short episodes.

Francesca, wife of Lanciotto, son of Malatesta, Lord of Rimini, is seen playing with her girl friends in the garden of her house. The scene changes and she is revealed reading a book at a table ; presently Paolo, Lanciotto's handsome brother, brings her flowers. He comes to her and they read together. They look up and kiss, then she runs to escape from him. He follows, enters her room, declares his love, and they " read no more."

At the same time, in another part of the stage, we see the return of Francesca's husband, clad in full armour. A servant tells him of his wife's unfaithfulness and his rage knows no bounds. The two scenes blend into one. He enters and slays the lovers.

The scene changes to Hell once more. Francesca having concluded her story, the unhappy couple soar again into their world of torment. The poet's tender heart cannot support the pathos of this sad tale and he falls fainting to the ground, or, as Dante says : *E caddi come corpo morto cade.*

**

The principal parts in this ballet were taken thus : Lubov Egorova (*Francesca*), Dubrovskaya (*Cleopatra*), Muromskaya (*Semiramis*), Barash (*Dido*), Spessivtzeva II (*Helen*), and T. Kshesinsky (*Dante*) ; B. Romanov (*Giovanni the Lame, son of Malatesta*), P. Vladimirov (*Paolo the Handsome, his brother*), A. Monakov (*Paris*), A. Medalinsky (*Tristan*), Ponomarov II (*Giovanni's servant*), Solainikov (*Virgil*).

III

Eros is an 1830 ballet adapted by Fokine from the story by V. Svetlov, entitled *A Fiesole Angel*. The music used consisted of the first, second, and third parts of Tchaikovsky's " Serenade for String Orchestra."

The scene shows a room with an open door leading on

to a garden, in which stands a statue of Eros. A young girl enters the room, escorted by her sweetheart. He bids her good-bye and gives her as a charm a little " Angel of Fiesole," which he has brought her from Italy. As he departs she throws him a farewell kiss.

Presently she reclines on the sofa and, composing herself, goes to sleep. She dreams that the winged Eros is looking at her. Soon he comes to her and she, frightened, imagines herself running with him in the garden.

Nymphs in ballet dresses of the Taglioni epoch enter and dance about Eros, who has returned to his pedestal, and decorate him with flowers. He bends down and kisses the girl. The Angel appears momentarily and the girl hesitates, but Eros draws her to him in a firm embrace. Again the Angel appears and this time hurls the god from his pedestal.

At this point the sleeping girl awakes with a start. But it is only the wind that has blown over the statue so that it lies in pieces on the ground. She goes to the sofa, takes the tiny Angel, hangs it on the wall, and kneels before it in prayer.

*
* *

The principal parts in this ballet were taken thus : Matilda Kshesinskaya (*Young Girl*), A. Vilzak (*Young Man*), P. Vladimirov (*Eros*), and F. Dubrovskaya (*The Angel*).

IV

Stenka Razin was arranged to Glazunov's well-known symphony of the same name. Stenka Razin was a Don Cossack, a leader of the people in revolt, who cruised about the Volga and the Caspian Sea and plundered with his band. At the moment when the ballet opens he has just landed on the shores of the Volga. His men roll out from the ship casks of wine, bring forth the spoils of their raids, and begin to divide the booty.

A Cossack dance follows which Stenka watches while he fondles his mistress, a captive Persian Princess. She dances for him, accompanied by her slaves. She loves her sinister master, but his men remark with anger that he loves her too, and seems to have lost his taste for the life into which he has drawn them.

They begin to mutiny and, surrounding him, roar their discontent. Suddenly he clutches one of them by the throat and slowly chokes the life out of the wretched man. The mutineers, abashed, carry away the dead body and murmur threateningly. Stenka orders the dance to continue, but frowns and broods, deep in thought.

Suddenly he picks up his mistress in his arms and walks on to the ship ; then, lifting her high above his head, he flings her into the river, saying : " Volga, take my dearest possession." His men doff their caps, appeased by this great sacrifice. But the Tsar's army approaches, there is no time to muse on the dead girl, and the whole band prepares to attack the Imperial forces.

* *
*

The principal parts in this ballet were taken thus : Vera Fokina (*Persian Princess*), Andreyev I (*Stenka Razin*), Solainikov, Monakov I, and B. Romanov (*Cossacks*).

In connection with the first production of this ballet an accident occurred which might have had serious consequences. When Andreyev (a singer of giant stature), in his character of Stenka Razin, lifted Vera Fokina, in her part of the Persian Princess, high above his head and then let her seemingly fall into the sea, Fokine arranged that a group of supers, hidden from the audience by the hull of the ship, should catch her in a cloth held by them, when they were to lay her on the floor and rush to the wings in readiness to dash upon the stage in simulation of an attack. As soon as the attack began, Fokine ran to the end wing to see his wife, only to find her unconscious on the floor and her maid bathing her forehead with cold water. After this incident the company urged Fokine to replace Fokina by a dummy, as the sheer drop from such a height was felt to be dangerous, and it was argued that the audience would not realise the difference. But Fokine, considering that this would detract from the effect of the ballet, did not agree, and so his wife continued to run this risk. When, however, the ballet was given later at Moscow, Fokine made use of a dummy, when his artistic fears were realised, for, owing to a movement of the dummy's wooden arm, the illusion was completely spoiled.

In addition to the three ballets mentioned, the programme contained a group of *divertissements*, also arranged by Fokine, the principal one being " *Bacchus*," danced by Fokine himself, which afterwards became a favourite number on his concert tours. The success of the whole performance was so great that Fokine was overwhelmed with requests to repeat the performance in aid of other charitable institutions. In all it was given three times. *Eros* was added to the repertory of the Imperial Theatres, but the two remaining ballets were left over for future consideration, as they required special scenery and a considerable number of new costumes.

V

The next year (1916) introduced two further productions : *Jota Aragonesa*[1] and *L'Apprenti Sorcier*, produced respectively at the Maryinsky Theatre on the 29th of January and the 15th of October.

The first, given for the benefit of the theatre orchestra, was the outcome of Fokine's travels in Spain. His study of the national dances on their native soil convinced him that Spanish ballets as given at the Imperial Theatres were far from correct, in steps, in rhythm, and in the line of the dancers. Furthermore, the " Spaniards " of the ballet were invariably sinister personages; the gaiety and the joy of life so characteristic of the genuine dances were completely absent from their dancing. Despite the name of the ballet, Fokine did not limit his choregraphic palette to the steps of the Jota, but introduced the elements of other Spanish dances.

The scenery, designed by Golovine, was, like the ballet, conceived in a very graceful, light and coquettish style. It represented a meadow gleaming in the sun with a background of snow-capped mountains ; and there were white costumes to suggest heat.

[1] The music is by Glazunov.

VI

The second ballet, given at a Charity Soirée of the Ladies' Circle of the Moscow Regiment of Life Guards, was arranged to the Scherzo " L'Apprenti Sorcier " by Paul Dukas, which is based on Goethe's ballad, " *Zauberlehring.*"

This is the story of the ballet which, it will be seen, is closely related to the ballad. A magician's pupil or apprentice seizes the opportunity of his master's absence to test the extent of his own powers. He draws a magic circle round a glowing brazier, mutters incantations, and makes cabalistic signs. Selecting his broom as an object for experiment he sends it on his own particular duty, that of drawing water from the well. The broom is represented by a dancer dressed in a manner to suggest this article ; his movements are grotesque and humorous. He sweeps the water—represented by a number of dancers— into the room. Now the neophyte wishes to stop the ceaseless rise of the water, but he has forgotten the all-important magic words. The water continues to rise carrying the furniture in all directions and finally nearly drowns the hapless pupil. But at the critical moment the old magician enters, pronounces the magic formula, and the water subsides and vanishes, whereupon the apprentice kneels before his saviour.

SCENE FROM " EROS "

MICHEL FOKINE AS THE MARQUIS IN " LE RÊVE DE LA
MARQUISE "

CHAPTER TWELVE

PRODUCTIONS IN MANY COUNTRIES

I

IN March, 1918, Fokine, accompanied by his wife and son, left Russia for Sweden, in accordance with an engagement to produce *Petrouchka* at the Royal Opera, Stockholm. Owing to a revolution in Finland, the journey lasted almost a whole month. The Fokines became stranded in Abo (Finland) and soon exhausted the money the Soviet authorities had allowed them to take for travelling expenses. While talking over their plight in a restaurant they got into conversation with a party of Russian officers dining nearby, one of whom recognised Fokine. As a result, arrangements were made immediately for two performances to be given by the Fokines, which were so successful that they were able to hire horse-sleighs and travel over the frozen sea to Stockholm. Unfortunately, when they did arrive, it was too late to produce *Petrouchka*.

Without either funds or engagement the Fokines were in a difficult situation; fortunately, however, they had brought their stage dresses with them. Thereupon, Fokine arranged a tour of Sweden and Denmark, which was so successful that in a few months the Fokines were able to live in their own house on the borders of Copenhagen. Seven performances were given at that city and the tour was extended to Norway. Fokine also gave lessons in dancing, first at Helsingfors[1], then at Charlotenlund[2], both in Denmark; pupils came from Norway, Sweden, Denmark, Germany, and Russia.

In the autumn Fokine went for two weeks to Stockholm, where, at the city Stadium, he gave two performances, on the 21st and 22nd of September, in which some 800 girls took part. The first consisted of four numbers called *The Four Seasons*: "*Spring*" (to the first part of Grieg's

[1] June to August 1918.
[2] June to September 1919.

" Peer Gynt Suite ") ; " *Summer* " (to Schumann's " Moment Musical ") ; " *Autumn* " (to Tchaikovsky's " Autumn Song ") ; and " *Winter* " (to the Snowflake Waltz from Tchaikovsky's " Casse Noisette Suite "). The third dance was the same as that created by Fokine for the Pupils' Performance in 1908, at the Theatre School, St. Petersburg. But, on the occasion of the Stockholm performance, the " leaves " were represented by 300 Swedish girls. At the second performance Fokine presented a choregraphic interpretation of Beethoven's " Moonlight Sonata."

II

Towards the end of 1919 Fokine went to America at the invitation of Morris Gest to produce at the Century Theatre, New York, the Bacchanale in *Aphrodite*, a spectacular musical play adapted from the well-known novel by Pierre Louÿs. This production, first performed on the 1st of December, had an immense success and ran for an entire season, when it was transferred to the Auditorium, Chicago. On the 30th of December, Fokine and his wife, the *prima ballerina* Vera Fokina, made their first personal appearance in America at the Metropolitan Opera House, New York, the programme including *Le Spectre de la Rose* and *Le Mort de Cygne*. This performance was repeated on the 10th of February (1920).

III

On the 1st of March, 1921, the Fokines again appeared at the Metropolitan Opera House, and on this occasion presented a new one-act ballet, *Le Rêve de la Marquise*. The music used was that written by Mozart to Noverre's charming theme *Les Petits Riens*, but Fokine's *scenario* was no less piquant. There are four characters only : The Marquise, played by Vera Fokina ; the Marquis and the Faun Awakened, a dual rôle taken by Michel Fokine ; and the Servant of the Marquise.

This is the story. The marquise, tired and heated from walking and dancing with her friend, the marquis, has an irresistible desire to loosen her heavy gown and take a cooling bath in a pool in the park. The marquis, after some pleading, finally agrees to leave her, and she sits down by the water to rest before bathing. Tired as she is, however, she falls asleep and has a terrifying dream.

In this dream the statue of a faun, the features of which greatly resemble those of the marquis, comes to life as soon as she begins to prepare herself for her bath. The marble statue, which has been standing in the old park for years without moving, inflamed with passion, pursues her frantically, and to escape she throws herself into the water. In triumphant glee, the faun shakes with laughter, and dances about the borders of the lake.

Then he takes her dress and hides it. The terrified marquise cries loudly for help. Her cries arouse the attendant, a little negro, who comes running to her rescue ; but the marquis-faun, who wishes to conceal his mistress's plight, smothers him with her own dress. Then the faun plunges into the water, seizes the frightened marquise in his arms, and covers her face with his caresses.

IV

On the 3rd of September, Fokine produced at the New York Hippodrome for the revue *Get Together*, a new ballet in one act, entitled *The Thunder Bird*, the theme adapted by Vera Fokina from an old Aztec legend. The music was an arrangement of selections from the works of Balakirev, Borodine, Glinka, Rimsky-Korsakov, and Tchaikovsky. The costumes were designed by Willy Pogany. The principal rôles were taken as follows : Vera Fokina (*The Thunder Bird, afterwards the Princess Nahua*), and Michel Fokina (*Aztlan, an Aztec Chief*).

Here is the synopsis as abstracted from the programme. " Returning from a successful hunt, Aztec warriors are performing ritual dances around sacrificial fires. Suddenly a violent storm breaks, which drives them to take refuge in the temple. Amidst the roaring thunder and flashes of lightning, a flock of ' thunder birds ' alight, led by Nahua, a beautiful Toltec Princess, who, by the wiles of a wicked

magician, has been changed into a bird. From the temple
door, Aztlan, the chief of the tribe, perceives the fluttering
and enchanted birds, and falls in love with Nahua. He
attempts to catch her, but she eludes him and flies away
with the others. Grieving at her departure, Aztlan calls
the Master of Mystic Forces, and asks him to capture the
beautiful bird by his magic.

"The Master with his attendants begins to cast the
spell, and suddenly there appears growing from the earth
a golden tree, whose branches entangle Nahua as she
comes flying through the air. Aztlan dashes towards the
struggling bird, but stops as if turned to stone by her
marvellous beauty. Hearing the birds' piercing cries, all
the warriors come running, and perceive that their chief
has been turned into a statue. They take their bows and
arrows and shoot at the birds. But at this moment Aztlan
comes to his senses, and throws himself before his loved
one to protect her. The arrows pierce his breast, and he
falls mortally wounded. He has sacrificed his life for
beauty. But the deed of love performs a miracle. The
tree begins to blossom with wonderful flowers, and opening
its branches, frees Nahua, who is restored as a beautiful
girl.

Approaching Aztlan, with tears of sorrow, she performs
a healing dance around him. He returns to life. The
Master of Mystic Forces unites the lovers and the whole
tribe, overjoyed, greets them with an Aztec war-dance."

v

In 1923, Fokine produced, on the 23rd of April, at the
New Amsterdam Theatre, New York, two new ballets for
the Ziegfeld Follies—*Frolicking Gods* and *Farljandio*.

The music for the first-named was Tchaikovsky's "Casse
Noisette Suite"; the scenery was designed by Joseph
Urban, and the costumes by John Reynolds. The principal
characters of the Girl and the Boy were taken respectively
by Martha Lorber and Serge Pernikov.

The theme, by M. Fokine, presumes that when the art
museums are closed the statues of the Greek gods which

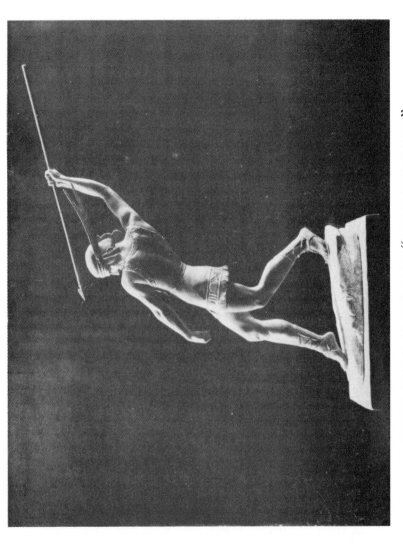

MICHEL FOKINE AS AZTLAN IN "THE THUNDER BIRD"
From the statuette by Harriet W. Frishmuth, 1921

MICHEL FOKINE AS PERSEUS IN " MEDUSA "

they contain come to life and take pleasure in dancing. Such a situation is imagined to take place in a Paris Art Museum in 1851, and the revels are witnessed by two lovers who are locked in the museum by chance. But a gendarme hears the terrible noise in the museum, finds the lovers undressed like the ancient Greeks, and takes them to the police station ; the statues have previously returned to their pedestals.

The theme of *Farljandio* was by John Reynolds, the music by V. Herbert. The scene is laid in the mountain town of Accio, the haunt of Sicilian gypsies, and the ballet is built around the Dance of Allurement which is danced by gypsy brides at their weddings.

VI

The year 1923 marked the twenty-fifth anniversary of Fokine's stage career, and on the 9th of May he was the recipient of a host of congratulatory messages, while at St. Petersburg, then become Petrograd, the occasion was celebrated by special performances of Fokine's ballets.

Below are two typical examples of the messages received, which it will be observed are full of gratitude and admiration for his artistic achievements, but express regret that he can no longer be with the company to act as their guide.

HONOURABLE MIKHAYL MIKHAYLOVICH,

The Management of the National Academic Theatres of Petrograd greets you on the twenty-fifth anniversary of your whole-hearted service to the art.

Petrograd is honouring you these days with the sincerest and greatest respect, just as if you were now among your friends and admirers. I take this happy opportunity of expressing to you my deep regret at your long absence and desire to remind you that for five years your fellow-workers have been upholding your artistic succession.

With sincerest respect,

*   *   *   *   *

ACTING DIRECTOR OF THE ACADEMIC THEATRES OF PETROGRAD.

DEAR MIKHAYL MIKHAYLOVICH,

The artistes of the Academic Ballet of Petrograd send you their sincerest greetings. All these five years we have felt that a dear person has been absent from our family, a great master and a great artist who once used to breathe fire into our hearts.

Indeed, we still have the perals of your artistic labour—many ballets which figure continually in the repertory—but their creator is not there, the one person necessary to restore those all-important details which we value so highly, and which we have endeavoured to preserve, but have failed and cannot restore without you.

Now that the conditions of life have considerably improved and there is an opportunity to work under normal circumstances, we should like to see you once more as our leader, creating new masterpieces and inspiring us with the belief in a new flowering of our art. As we celebrate our festival, the greatest event in our lives, your twenty-fifth anniversary, we feel your absence more deeply than ever.

Dear Mikhayl Mikhaylovich, come back, return to your family, we miss you so much.

Signed by
THE COMMITTEE OF THE ACADEMIC BALLET OF PETROGRAD.

VII

On the 26th of September, Fokine produced at the Empire Theatre, New York, a ballet-pantomime called *The Return from the Carnival*, which was used as a choregraphic prologue to the play *Casanova*, by Lorenzo de Azertis.

In the autumn Fokine went to London to arrange the dances in Basil Dean's production of Flecker's play *Hassan*, which was first produced at His Majesty's Theatre on the 20th of September. There were three dances. First, an excellent beggars' dance, very interesting for its grotesque movements. Then, an Eastern dance executed to the rhythmic clapping of hands which abruptly changed to a frenzied measure reminiscent of the finale to the *Polovtsian Dances from Prince Igor*. Lastly, there was a stirring sword dance in the Trial Scene.

VIII

The following year (1924) the Fokines organised their "American Ballet," composed of a picked company of their pupils. The first performance was given on the 26th of February, at the Metropolitan Opera House, New

York, and included three new ballets—*Elves, Medusa,* and
Ole Toro.

***

Elves was arranged to Mendelssohn's " Overture to
A Midsummer Night's Dream " and to the same com-
poser's Andante and Allegro from the " Violin Concerto
(Op. 64)."

***

Medusa was a ballet-tragedy arranged to Tchaikovsky's
" Symphonie Pathétique." There are four characters :
Medusa, Perseus, Poseidon, and Pallas. The first and
second parts were taken by Vera Fokina and Michel Fokine
respectively.

This is the theme. According to an ancient Greek
legend, the sea god Poseidon fell in love with Medusa, the
beautiful, and induced her to transgress upon the sanctity
of the Temple of Pallas. The chaste goddess punished
Medusa by changing her into a snake-haired monster,
whose very glance would turn to stone whatever it was
cast upon. Many gallant warriors perished in the attempt
to fight Medusa until Perseus's bravery and craft conquered the monster. Using his shield as a mirror, he
hypnotised Medusa by her own reflection, and cut off her
head.

***

Ole Toro was a ballet-intermede arranged to music by
Rimsky-Korsakov. There are three principal characters :
Inesilla, Torrereo, and El Jeloso ; the first two were
taken by Vera Fokina and Fokine respectively. The solo
dances are set against a background of boys and girls of
Seville.

The theme is an interesting one. Young people gathered
together in a tavern begin a practical joke : they make the
target of their fun a jealous lover, whose angry gestures
recall to their mind the behaviour of a bull in the arena.
Soon a mock bull-fight is started which brings the anger
of the jealous youth to the boiling point. He becomes
even threatening, and only the charm, beauty, and dances

127

of Inesilla manage to appease his mood and bring the episode to a happy conclusion.

IX

Fokine's " American Ballet " toured the principal cities of the United States with success, and on the occasion of a series of three performances given on August 17th, 18th, and 19th, at the Lewisohn Stadium, College of the City of New York, the average number of spectators at each performance exceeded 14,000 !

In the late autumn Fokine went to London to produce the dances in Basil Dean's production of Shakespeare's *A Midsummer Night's Dream*, first performed on Boxing Night (December 26th), at the Theatre Royal, Drury Lane.

Photo : Wide World Studio, New York

A GROUP FROM FOKINE'S BALLET "ELVES"

Photograph taken during a rehearsal at his studio, Riverside Drive, New York

Photo : Semo, Mexico

MICHEL FOKINE
From a photograph taken shortly before his fatal illness in 1942

CHAPTER THIRTEEN
CONCLUSION

IN this book I have sought to present an account of Fokine's choregraphic achievements over a period of some twenty years.

When one delves into the past and seeks to ascertain what a ballet by an old master was like, nothing is more difficult to find than a description which affords some idea of the movements of the dancers and of the development of the action on the stage. For this reason the more important ballets have been described at length in the hope not only of evoking memories of great days that are past, but of preserving to posterity at least a faint impression of some of Fokine's masterpieces.

Fokine's contribution to the art of choregraphy has been of immense service in elevating the art of ballet to new heights, and in both leading and pointing out the way to new experiments. The amount of work accomplished by Fokine has probably never been equalled except by Marius Petipa. And it is quantity matched with quality, for almost any one of such ballets as *Les Sylphides*, *Le Carnaval*, *Petrouchka*, *Le Spectre de la Rose*, and *Schéhérazade*, would have sufficed to procure its author undying fame.

I have been privileged to watch Fokine at rehearsal, and followed with absorbing interest the shaping of a ballet at his hands. He comes to the rehearsal-room with almost every detail in his mind ; he requires only dancers to bring before us the phantom pictures and movements that people his brain. He knows what phrase of music is to be interpreted in such a movement, when there is to be a pose, and for how long. He composes like a painter, sketching a few movements here, arranging a few details of a pose there ; it is one of the most entrancing experiences to see these apparently isolated elements gradually set in their proper order and combined to form a beautiful dance. The sensation received can only be compared to the witnessing of a film of a growing flower.

A point of particular interest regarding Fokine's ballets is their perennial youthfulness and freshness. Every new artistic fad and musical fashion has produced its crop of marvels destined to accomplish who knows what new revolution in choreographic art, only to disappear into the limbo of forgotten things. Yet many of Fokine's ballets are given all over the world year after year with unfailing regularity and undiminished popularity. In 1934 it was possible to see in London alone three different productions of *Le Carnaval* and *Les Sylphides*.

But the familiar words "choreography by Michel Fokine" which figure so frequently in programmes of ballet must not always be taken too literally. A revival produced from memory by a former dancer in one of Fokine's ballets, or produced partly from memory and partly from seeing another revival, often bears only a faint resemblance to the original. There are few scruples at devising something to fill in what has been forgotten. And when the basic movements are correct, how often is the vital quality of movement completely lacking. Worse still, I have seen the whole conception of a character changed completely.

Two other points bearing on this matter should be taken into consideration. Fokine's ballets are composed with careful thought for the abilities of the artistes at his disposal, and with due regard for the costumes the dancers are to wear and the setting in which they are to appear. Now many of Fokine's ballets have been composed with artist-dancers of the first rank, consequently, when the artistes presenting a Fokine composition are of lesser quality than the original creators of the various rôles, the ballet suffers a corresponding loss in effect. *Le Spectre de la Rose*, for instance, danced by Karsavina and Nijinsky in the flower of their art, is one thing, the same miniature ballet rendered by dancers of average ability produces a quite different impression.

Again, some revivals have been provided with new costumes and new scenery with the result that certain movements and patterns expressly designed to produce a particular colour effect completely lose their significance.

It is of the utmost importance that these facts should be known, *for only those who have seen the original ballets as they left the hands of their creator* can appreciate fully what a work of art a Fokine ballet can be.

Fokine has exerted a profound and beneficial influence on every branch of the art of ballet. He has instituted important reforms in ballet costume ; he has made mime in ballet expressive in place of the former series of conventional gestures ; he has proved the importance of using good music ; he has stressed the necessity for a dance to conform to the theme ; he has insisted on correct style-atmosphere. To glance at this list of his achievements is to be reminded of Noverre. The analogy is not inapposite, for Fokine has every right to be termed the Noverre of the twentieth century.

APPENDICES

A. FOKINE'S THEORIES ON THE ART OF BALLET
  (*a*) *The New Ballet.*
  (*b*) *Letter to " The Times," July 6th,* 1914.
  (*c*) *Not although, but because . . . !*

B. RECEPTION OF FOKINE'S BALLETS BY THE LONDON
    PRESS.

C. SUMMARY OF THE ACTIVITIES OF MICHEL FOKINE
    DURING THE PERIOD 1918–1931.

APPENDIX A

FOKINE'S THEORIES ON THE ART OF BALLET

(a) THE NEW BALLET

(Translated from the article contributed by Fokine to the Russian periodical, *Argus*, No. 1, 1916).

1. ON BALLET ROUTINE

Before I discuss the traditions which hinder the natural development of the art of ballet, I wish to state that I shall consider what in my opinion is wrong. But I shall deal with laws and traditions, and not with the talents of the artistes. It must be admitted that the creators of the old ballet possessed genius which, however, was restricted by unnecessary rules. The traditional ballet forgot man's natural beauty. It essayed to express a psychological feeling by a fixed movement, or series of movements, which could neither describe nor symbolise anything.

Not only did the spectators fail to understand the expressions of the artistes, but one artiste did not know what another was supposed to convey to him. The audience witness a number of movements but never trouble to question whether they are expressive. Some of these are familiar to them from long acquaintance. For example, it is understood that when a dancer points one finger upwards and then touches his lips with it, he is entreating a kiss ; it is curious that in all ballets only one kiss is requested. If the girl to whom he makes this sign runs away from him, proudly raises her arms, points to herself, lowers her arms in front of her and then sweeps them to one side, it is intended to intimate that her would-be lover is rich while she is poor, and consequently he would soon cast her away. This incident is repeated in *Paquita*, *Esmeralda*, and *La Bayadère*. But this series of gestures cannot even pretend to be expressive. It is hardly likely that a man desirous of obtaining a kiss would point with his finger ; but that is the traditional method of making love in a ballet. The expressiveness of the action is relatively unimportant, it is the beauty of the poses and movements, the graceful action of pointing one finger to Heaven that is all important.

Then there is the famous gesture where a man raises the right hand and sweeps it in a circular movement about his face. This is supposed to convey to the audience that his sweetheart is beautiful. But does it really mean anything? If you follow such a scene in a ballet it is easy to observe that both artistes and audience are indifferent to these signs which, in fact, are only employed as a means of filling up so many bars of the music. Consider *Le Lac des Cygnes*. Siegfried's tutor comes on the stage and says: " Benno is coming here." The latter enters and remarks: " Siegfried is coming here." Then Siegfried enters, greets the peasants and his friends, drinks some wine and begins to talk. What does he say? " My mother is coming here." In this way several pages of music are disposed of. In many ballets the newcomer says: " I have come here." Surely his presence is sufficiently obvious. But follow the appearance of Siegfried's mother, a character who seems inseparable from so many ballets. When she appears on the scene, she circles round the stage; but can any mother explain why she does this? Then she begs her son to renounce drinking and marry. She clasps her hands and entreats: " Please marry." He replies: " No ! " She repeats: " Please marry." He replies again: " No ! " She beseeches him for the third time and he consents. Is it not clear that such a dialogue is possible only as a result of the complete absence of expressive signs in ballet, for if these signs were comprehensible, so that the audience was interested in the logic of the scene, it could not take place? But expressive signs are replaced by fixed movements which none can understand.

II. The Development of Signs

I have mentioned the above details because, in my opinion, a dance is the development and ideal of the sign. The ballet renounced expession and consequently dancing became acrobatic, mechanical, and empty. In order to restore dancing its soul we must abandon fixed signs and devise others based on the laws of natural expression. " But," it may be asked, " how can a dance be built on a sign? " Consider the *arabesque* of the good old times. " But," it may be argued, " you employed *arabesques* in *Les Sylphides*." Certainly, an *arabesque* is sensible when it idealises the sign, because it suggests the body's straining to soar upward, the whole body is expressive. If there be no expression, no sign, but merely a foot raised in the position

136

termed *en arabesque*, it looks foolish. That is the difference between the good old, and the merely old.

Examine the prints of Cerrito, Grisi, Ellsler, and Taglioni, it will be found that their poses have a certain expressiveness. Now look through a history of dancing, on the concluding pages of which will be found the dancers of the end of the last century. Their poses are quite different. There is no sign. What does their pose express ? Simply a leg extended backwards. It is neither the beginning nor end of the sign, nor its development. Instead of expressing something, the body seeks balance to avoid falling on account of the raised leg.

There is a vast difference between the dancers of the beginning of the nineteenth century, when the ballet reached its height in beauty, and those at the end of the century, when beauty was forced to give place to acrobatics. There is a complete difference in principle. Taglioni raises herself *sur les pointes* in order to be so light as to seem hardly to touch the ground. The dancer of the period when ballet was in decline uses her *pointes* in order to astonish the audience with their strength and endurance. She fills up the toe of her satin shoe and jumps on it so that the shoe hits the ground with all the strength of her muscular feet. The " steel " toe is a horrible invention of the ballet in decline. In its days of greatness, supernatural lightness was the ideal. Now, the steel toe, hard legs, and precision in execution, are the ideals.

III. The Old and the New in Ballet. The Creative Power in Ballet

I ask for the careful preservation of the beauty of the dance as Taglioni knew it. That world of fragile dreams could not support the rude acrobatic ballet and has fled from us. It will never return if we do not exert all our strength to save this highest form of the dance. But, having preserved it, this style must be employed only when it is applicable. No single form of dancing should be adopted once and for all. The best form is that which most fully expresses the meaning desired, and the most natural one that which most closely corresponds with the idea to be conveyed. For example, ballet steps executed *sur la pointe* cannot be used in a Greek Bacchic dance, on the other hand it would be unnatural to dance a Spanish dance in a Greek *chiton*.

If the music be in character with Spanish folk melodies and

rhythms, the dance must also express the same national character. Climate and history have created the temperament which naturally gave birth to those particular forms. The rhythmic tapping of the heel, the sensuous swaying of the whole body, the snake-like movement of the arms, are more natural in this case than the most natural dance of the barefoot school. Whatever the period required by the theme, the ballet must always create a dance which correspondingly expresses that period. I do not wish to imply by this an ethnological accuracy or archæological exactitude ; but there must be co-ordination of style and movement with the style of the period.

Man has always changed his plastic language. He has expressed in the most varied forms his sorrows, his joys, and all the emotions he experienced, hence his mode of expression cannot be fixed according to any one rule. The old method of production consisted in creating dances from fixed movements and poses, the mimed scenes were always expressed by a fixed manner of gesticulation, and thus the audience had to understand the theme. The most prominent creators of ballet were bound hand and foot by those laws and traditions. We must denounce this. Work of this kind is very easy for the producer and the artistes, and lightens the work of the critic. It is easy to judge whether a dancer has executed correctly the steps which he or she has performed a hundred times in other ballets. But there is one drawback to this method, a ready-made pattern does not always fit.

IV. CONFUSION

Creators of ballets should always endeavour to seek out that form of dancing which best expresses the particular theme, for this principle leads to great beauty. However varied the rule of ballet might become, life would always be more varied still ; while ballet having no relation to reality and circumscribed by tradition naturally becomes ludicrous. The old ballet has confused periods and styles. It uses Russian top-boots and the French school of dancing in one ballet, the short ballet-skirt and historically correct Egyptian costume in another, and so forth. Is not that confusion ? The style of the dance is always inharmonious with that of the costumes, theme, and period. Moreover, there is one style for classical dances, another for character dances ; and all these appear in one ballet and at the same time. Such is tradition. And to give one homogeneous, harmonious thing is to sin against it, because in order to comply with ballet æsthetics it is imperative to reproduce dual styles.

V. BALLET RULES

The classical ballet came into being as a pleasure of the aristocracy and part of court ceremony. The bowing before the public, the addressing of hand movements to them, and so on, are the foundations on which the rules of ballet were built. Examine the photographs of academic dancers in, for instance, a *pas de deux*; the *danseur* always stands behind the *danseuse*. He holds her waist and looks at her back, while she faces the audience. He displays her. If I do not agree with this style of dancing, it does not mean that I ignore the school. On the contrary, I think that in order to create anything of value one must study and pass through a proper school which, however, should not be confined to the study of fixed poses and steps.

First, one must study oneself, conquer one's own body, and try to learn to feel and develop an ability to perform various movements. Ballet gymnastics are limited, they do not develop the whole body nor instil a feeling for pose and movement in all their variety. The ballet at the end of the last century was limited to several rules handed down without explanation as dogmas. It was of no avail to inquire the why and the wherefore because no one could answer such questions, they were too old. One had to accept the creed that the feet should keep to the five positions and that all movements consisted in combinations of these positions; that the arms should be rounded, the elbows held sideways facing the audience, the back straight, and the feet turned outwards with the heels well to the front. It is difficult to lose faith in these five positions in order to realise that beauty of movement cannot be limited by them.

The practice of turning the legs outward certainly develops the flexibility of the lower limbs, but exercises *en dehors* develop the feet to one side only. In order to make sure it is sufficient to look at a dancer with turned out feet in a dance requiring the feet to be in a natural position. It is obvious that she is ill at ease. Her feet are not under control. I appreciate the " turning out " of the feet in preliminary exercises, but as soon as the exercises are finished the " turning out " should cease, except in Siamese, Hindu, and exotic dances, when the feet should harmonise with the angular positions of the arms. But a barefoot dance with the feet turned out is absurd.

Another failing of ballet technique is that it is concentrated in the dancing of the lower limbs, whereas the whole body should dance. The whole body to the smallest muscle should be expressive, but ballet schools concentrate on exercises for the feet. The arms are limited to a few movements and the hands to one fixed position. What variety would not be possible if the dancer renounced the mannerism of rounded arms. And the movement of the upper part of the body, to what does that lead? A straight back, that is the ideal. One must be deaf not to become furious when the teacher continually repeats for eight or nine years one and the same rule—hold up your back. What store of beauty have painters not taken from the different positions of the body? The academic dancer, however, always faces the audience in a straight line.

The conservative critics were furious because the dancers in certain of my ballets wore sandals and Eastern shoes, and only used the traditional ballet-shoe in some ballets. The admirers of academic dancing could not understand the view that *pointes* should be used as a means and not as the sole aim of ballet. *Pointes* should be employed where they are suitable and renounced without regret where they would not serve any artistic purpose. For instance, in Eastern ballets, the bare foot or a soft shoe is more pleasing than a ballet-shoe, but the dancer in *Le Cygne* does not offend when she uses her *pointes* to suggest a soaring movement. It is right if all her body express the same feeling, but wrong if she use her *pointes* to display her " steel " toe. She degrades herself before the audience which is watching for the strength of her toes. It is a complete misunderstanding of this beautiful mode of progression.

Forgetful of its artistic aims, ballet began to use *pointes* for quite opposite means, in fact merely to display the endurance and strength of the toes. The shoe was filled up with leather, cotton wool, and cork. But this did not make any difference to anyone, because a competition began as to who could make the most turns *sur la pointe*. The dancer's toes became ugly and it became impossible for her to show her foot without the shoe. That also did not matter. If we admit that ballet should develop mime for most styles of dancing, the basis of the school should be the teaching of natural movement. One should be able to move naturally and control the body to this end. The natural dance should follow and then one could advance to the dance of artificial movement. Ballet however begins at the end. It renounces natural movement, but surely the ballet has no right to discard what it did not possess. Vrubel had the right to paint a mutilated demon because he could draw a beautiful human body.

VI. Basic Movements

There are very few dancers who can walk and run about naturally. At first, when I asked a dancer not to execute *pas de bourrée* but simply run, she would become shy and say : " No, I cannot." But dancing is developed from these basic movements. The natural dance is built on raising the foot backwards and forwards just as in the action of walking. The ballet, however, abounds in sideway movements. The so-called second position, so inæsthetic, is the one most used in academic dancing. What could be more ugly and vulgar than the feet wide apart. But many steps are built on it, such as *glissade, échappé*, and so forth. The chief reason for it is because ballet is danced mostly facing the public, whom the dancer respects and from whom he or she awaits approval. If it be agreed that every pose should express the inner self, that every movement should be logical, then it is obvious that sideway movements are senseless, expressionless, and ugly.

Gautier, who lived in the period of the highest development of the classic ballet, was very much opposed to the " turned out " dance. Is it not strange that this turned out dance is championed by so many admirers of the classical ballet ?

VII. Delightful Nonsense

The step from the senseless to the expressive dance does not lead to cheap drama, to the narrow dramatisation of the dance ; it expresses everything that is in the human soul. " Why," it is argued, " should ballet contain expression and drama when it should be unreal and irrational ? " Someone has styled ballet " delightful nonsense." I am glad that ballet is considered " delightful," but if it were not nonsense it would have gained. Expression is as necessary to ballet as any other art, even more so. If colours and sounds do not speak they are tolerable, but an expressionless human body resembles a doll or a corpse. In pictures we look for the painter's soul. We do not accept a picture which expresses nothing ; how then can we tolerate a man without expression ?

If ballet forsake its direct aim for expression, the result is that one part expresses one thing, and the other the opposite. The most typical example is the *jouetté*. For me this is the most hateful invention of the ballet. The dancer expresses ecstasy and joy, but her face—what does that express? Quite the opposite. She seeks for balance and the whole face proclaims it. The body is straight, the head also, the hands are symmetrical, the eyes fixed on one point. The face betrays her fear of losing her balance. There are few who can watch the expression of her features while she moves ; what a contradiction ! Unity of pose and movement is a law which, to my regret, is not felt by everybody. This can only be explained by the undeveloped ability to seize quickly poses and movements.

VIII. ACROBATISM

What is the difference between a dancer who executes thirty-two pirouettes and an acrobat who performs twice as many ? I think that an acrobat does his with more certainty, but there should be another difference. Everything that an acrobat does is for the purpose of effect, to astonish, to amuse, and establish a record. This is in the nature of sport which element should be quite foreign to the ballet. The aim of every movement in ballet should be expression. A dancer representing a satyr can do somersaults, roll on the ground, and, if he conveys the impression that he is half-man, half-animal, he has fulfilled his mission as an artist. But if a dancer representing a princess turns like a top, she must renounce all pretence of being an artist. The impression given would be strong but of a quite different character.

Just as acrobats have broken bones, so ballet dancers have " turned out " feet. If this were æsthetic, this form of beauty would long ago have been revealed to us by painters. Let us examine the best works of sculpture and painting from the point of view of a *maître de ballet* of the old school. All the marble gods of Greece would appear in faulty poses, since none of them have " turned out " feet or hold their arms in ballet positions. All the figures of Rodin, Michaelangelo, Raphael, and the Renaissance period would be incorrect. And to be a true follower of classical ballet we should denounce all the treasures of beauty stored for thousands of years by man's genius and declare them to be wrong.

I am far from desirous of laying down any rules prohibiting certain forms of dance and mime. I even admit that a figure with " turned out " feet can be interesting and beautiful, if it be the product of a national or exotic character so that the whole figure harmonise with " turned out " feet and arms, such as may be observed in the statues adorning Indian temples. The natural position of the body is the point of departure for all styles and it would be a mistake to renounce the possibilities of the artificial dance. Observe Indian sculpture, the figures of ancient Assyria, Babylon, Egypt, and Greece, poetical Persian miniatures, Japanese and Chinese water-colours. All these depict unnatural movements and are opposed to the theory of the free and natural dance, but they possess so much beauty, such variety of style, and express the ideals of the various nationalities. How then can we sacrifice this variety for a fixed formula ? The artist of the dance should admit the life and art of all humanity and not confine himself to a few poor rules and old-fashioned traditions of the ballet school.

(*b*) LETTER TO " THE TIMES," JULY 6TH, 1914.

To the Editor of " The Times."

Sir—I am extremely grateful to the English Press for the attention which it has given to the " Russian Ballet," now appearing at Drury Lane Theatre, but at the same time I should like to point out certain misconceptions which exist as to the history of that ballet and the principles on which it is founded.

The misconceptions are these, that some mistake this new school of art, which has arisen only during the last seven years, for the traditional ballet which continues to exist in the Imperial theatres of St. Petersburg and Moscow, and others mistake it for a development of the principles of Isadora Duncan, while as a matter of fact the new Russian ballet is sharply differentiated by its principles both from the older ballet and from the art of that great dancer.

THE OLD CONVENTIONS

The older ballet developed the form of so-called " classical dancing," consciously preferring to every other form the artificial form of dancing on the point of the toe, with the feet turned out, in short bodices, with the figure tightly laced in stays, and with a strictly-established system of steps, gestures, and attitudes. Miss Duncan rejected the ballet and established an entirely opposite form of her own. She introduced natural dancing, in which the body of the dancer was liberated not only from stays and satin slippers, but also from the dance-steps of the ballet. She founded her dancing on natural movements and on the most natural of all dance-forms—namely, the dancing of the ancient Greeks.

The new ballet, which also rejects the conventions of the older ballet, cannot nevertheless be regarded as a follower of Miss Duncan. Every form of dancing is good in so far as it expresses the content or subject with which the dance deals ; and that form is the most natural which is most suited to the purpose of the dancer. It would be equally unnatural to represent a Greek Bacchic dance with ballet-steps on the point of the toes, or to represent a characteristic Spanish national dance by running and jumping in a Greek tunic and falling into attitudes copied from paintings on ancient Greek vases. No one form of dancing should be accepted once and for all.

Borrowing its subjects from the most various historical periods, the ballet must create forms corresponding to the various periods represented. I am not speaking of ethnographical or archæological exactitude, but of the correspondence of the style of the dancing and gestures with the style of the periods represented. In the course of the ages man has repeatedly changed his plastic language and expressed his joys and sorrows and all his emotions under a great variety of forms, often of extreme beauty. For man is infinitely various, and the manifold expressiveness of his gestures cannot be reduced to a single formula.

The art of the older ballet turned its back on life and on all the other arts and shut itself up in a narrow circle of traditions. According to the old method of producing a ballet, the ballet-master composed his dances by combining certain well-established movements and poses, and for his mimetic scenes he used a conventional system of gesticulation, and endeavoured by gestures of the dancers' hands according to established rules to convey the plot of the ballet to the spectator.

THE NEW IDEAS

In the new ballet, on the other hand, the dramatic action is expressed by dances and mimetic in which the whole body plays a part. In order to create a stylistic picture the ballet-master of the new school has to study, in the first place, the national dances of the nations represented, dances differing immensely from nation to nation, and often expressing the spirit of a whole race ; and, in the second, the art and literature of the period in which the scene is laid. The new ballet, while recognizing the excellence both of the older ballet, and of the dancing of Isadora Duncan in every case where they are suitable to the subject to be treated, refuses to accept any one form as final and exclusive.

· If we look at the best productions of sculptural and pictorial art from the point of view of a choreographer of the old school thoroughly versed in the rules of traditional gesticulation and of dancing with the toes turned out we shall find that the marble gods of Greece stood in entirely wrong attitudes ; not one of them turned his toes out or held his hands in the positions required by the rules of ballet dancing. Equally faulty from the old-fashioned ballet-master's point of view are the majestic statues of Michael Angelo and the expressive figures in the paintings of the Renaissance, to say nothing of the creations of

Raphael and of all modern art from Rodin down. If we are to be true to the rules of the older ballet we must turn our backs on the treasures of beauty accumulated by the genius of mankind during thousands of years, and declare them all to be wrong.

If we look from the point of view of the natural dancing of Miss Duncan, the fantastic attitudes of statues which adorn the temples of India, the severely beautiful figures of ancient Egypt, Assyria, and Babylon, the poetic miniatures of Persia, the water-colours of Japan and China, the art of prehistoric Greece, of the popular chap-books and broadsides of Russia—all alike are far removed from the natural movements of man, and cannot be reconciled with any theory of free and natural dancing. And yet they contain an immense store of beauty, an immense variety of taste, and are clear expressions of the character and ideals of the various nations which produced them. Have we any right to reject all this variety for the sake of adherence to a single formula ? No.

THE FIVE PRINCIPLES

Not to form combinations of ready-made and established dance-steps, but to create in each case a new form corresponding to the subject, the most expressive form possible for the re-presentation of the period and the character of the nation represented—that is the first rule of the new ballet.

The second rule is that dancing and mimetic gesture have no meaning in a ballet unless they serve as an expression of its dramatic action, and they must not be used as a mere diver-tissement or entertainment, having no connection with the scheme of the whole ballet.

The third rule is that the new ballet admits the use of con-ventional gesture only where it is required by the style of the ballet, and in all other cases endeavours to replace gestures of the hands by mimetic of the whole body. Man can be and should be expressive from head to foot.

The fourth rule is the expressiveness of groups and of en-semble dancing. In the older ballet the dancers were ranged in groups only for the purpose of ornament, and the ballet-master was not concerned with the expression of any sentiment in groups of characters or in ensemble dances. The new ballet, on the other hand, in developing the principle of ex-pressiveness, advances from the expressiveness of the face to

146

the expressiveness of the whole body, and from the expressiveness of the individual body to the expressiveness of a group of bodies and the expressiveness of the combined dancing of a crowd.

The fifth rule is the alliance of dancing with other arts. The new ballet, refusing to be the slave either of music or of scenic decoration, and recognizing the alliance of the arts only on the condition of complete equality, allows perfect freedom both to the scenic artist and to the musician. In contradistinction to the older ballet it does not demand " ballet music " of the composer as an accompaniment to dancing ; it accepts music of every kind, provided only that it is good and expressive. It does not demand of the scenic artist that he should array the ballerinas in short skirts and pink slippers. It does not impose any specific " ballet " conditions on the composer or the decorative artist, but gives complete liberty to their creative powers.

These are the chief rules of the new ballet. If its ideals have not yet been fully realized, its purpose has at any rate been declared plainly enough to split not only the public and the Press but also the members of the St. Petersburg ballet, into two opposing groups, and has led to the establishment of that " Russian Ballet " which visits all foreign countries and is often mistaken for the traditional Russian Ballet which still continues its existence in Moscow and St. Petersburg.

No artist can tell to what extent his work is the result of the influence of others and to what extent it is his own. I cannot, therefore, judge to what extent the influence of the old traditions is preserved in the new ballet and how much the new ideals of Miss Duncan are reflected in it. In accordance with the principles of the new ballet which I have set out above, in composing the ballets which (together with the old ballet, *Le Lac des Cygnes*) constitute the repertory of the " Russian Ballet " at Drury Lane I was not only under the influence of the artists of the historical periods represented, but deliberately sought that influence. When I composed an ancient Greek ballet I studied the artists of ancient Greece ; when I produced *Le Coq d'Or* I studied the old Russian chap-books and broadsides ; and when I produced *Schéhérazade*, *Cleopatra*, *Le Spectre de la Rose*, and the Polovtsian dances in *Prince Igor*, in each case I made use of different materials appropriate to the ballet in hand.

Yours faithfully,

MICHEL FOKINE.

(6) NOT ALTHOUGH, BUT BECAUSE . . . !

A Dialogue with Michel Fokine.

Recorded by DR. PIERRE TUGAL.

[The following Dialogue, written by Dr. Pierre Tugal, Keeper of the *Archives Internationales de la Danse*, and based on his recent conversation with Fokine, was first published in the journal of the A.I.D., January, 1934.]

The Orator.—Sir, I salute you in the name of all the dancers of France and Navarre. And I . . .

A Distinguished Man of Letters.—And I beg of you to tell me first of all whether Isadora Duncan has had as great an influence as is asserted.

Fokine.—I was a sincere admirer of Isadora Duncan, and, up till now, I still ponder with amazement on the sublime gospel of natural beauty expounded by that priestess of the Dance. Did she influence me? That is for others to say; personally, I do not think so, since, long before her *début* in Russia, I had offered to the directorate of the Imperial Theatres the synopsis of Daphnis and Chloë, specifying that a Greek ballet requires a plastic form of choregraphy. And how do you think my suggestion was received! I was proclaimed a heretic. Yet my work is rather the contrary of Isadora Duncan's teaching.

A Bachelor from Salamanca.—That is most inadequate. Be good enough to develop your thesis.

Fokine.—For Isadora Duncan, the uttermost beauty of Dancing is the pure glory of movement. For me, that is only the beginning. It is imperative to go further and idealise movement. In Dancing, one should never rest content with what is natural. Is not the purpose of Art to perfect life from the standpoint of exaltation of Beauty and expression? Just as singing is the idealisation of the voice, so dancing is the exaltation of movement, but always in harmony with Nature's laws. Before Duncan came, there was a period when the idea of truth in all that concerns ballet had been completely lost. It was Duncan who brought dancing back to its true beginnings. That was her great merit, just as it was her mistake to stop half-way.

A Bibliophile.—All that, my dear sir, was not enough to attack the old ballet with such force as to destroy it.

148

Fokine.—The old ballet had fallen into a fatal error due to its routine and artificial practices. There was always too great a gap between the theme and the stage action. The latter was explained by means of inexpressive traditional dances, while, to make the plot more comprehensible, recourse was had to a form of gesticulation based on the most conventional actions. Hence the spectators were offered a tedious double problem. Moreover, each ballet consisted in reality of a series of dances which could be transferred without injury to other ballets, to which they were equally well suited.

A Rich Patroness.—And you were disgusted . . .

Fokine.—I was disgusted with that routine. In my opinion, mime should be sometimes natural, sometimes stylised, and even conventional, as required by the theme. But it is imperative that the style should be in harmony with the theme of the ballet. The first essential is that the choregraphic and musical themes should be simultaneously expressed in dancing and mime in harmony with the action.

The Same Lady.—That was quite new !

Fokine.—Yes, it was new then ; however, in the end I was able to enforce my views, put them into practice, and, so it is said, my efforts have been crowned with success.

The Reporter.—In short, what then is your principle ?

Fokine.—That each ballet demands a new technique appropriate to its style.

The Man of Letters.—No—joking apart !

Fokine.—A new technique !

So-and-So.—What is a classical ballet in reality ?

A Balletomane.—Why a ballet in which there is dancing *sur les pointes* and in which traditional *pas* are used !

Fokine.—That is a quite erroneous definition. *Pointes* do not make a classical ballet. Thus, in all my many ballets, there are not ten even in which I have made use of *pointes*, and hardly any in which I have had recourse to the five positions.

The Reporter.—Yes, but many people blame you for not being a hundred per cent. classicist.

Fokine.—For those who consider that a classical ballet must consist on the one hand of a conventional system of mime, and, on the other, of traditional steps, that is to say, *pas* or daily exercises transferred to the stage, for those, I say, my ballets are not classical. In fact, I desire unity of action and I seek to express it through the movements of the whole body ; I no

149

longer divide ballet into mime and dancing. I make dancing expressive and mime rhythmic.

The Bibliophile.—However, everyone looks upon you as the most eminent composer of classical ballets.

Fokine.—You are too flattering ! If a classical ballet be one in which the dancers of both sexes are forced to employ all the resources of an accepted, time-honoured technique, then my ballets are classical.

The Rich Patroness.—Then you favour the traditional technique ? I should say the out-of-date technique ?

Fokine.—The dancer should know how to move his body in the most perfect manner. He can only achieve this by having a thorough knowledge of classical ballet technique which is the outcome of centuries of experience and which, moreover, is still being perfected by the Russian school.

An Enquirer after Knowledge.—Do you think that technique can have a detrimental effect on expressive dancing ?

Fokine.—Quite the contrary ; a dancer, possessed of a good traditional technique, has many more means of expression at his disposal than dancers not so trained. Knowledge does not imply limitation.

An Enquirer after Knowledge.—But schools which are opposed to technique, have they not produced many new steps and gestures ?

Fokine.—I have carefully observed the dancers produced by such schools and I can easily show that there is not a single one of their movements which has not already been used by us, and that every dancer trained in classical ballet technique is capable of dancing in what is termed a modernist ballet.

The Rich Patroness.—You hold a brief for the school you admire. However, I have seen a great deal that is new.

Fokine.—For the person who knows little, everything which he sees for the first time can appear new. The grotesque, which is so fashionable at present, is nothing new in ballet, This style has been in use for a very long while and employed much more skilfully, and, above all, where it was appropriate and not on every possible occasion.

The Rich Patroness.—However that may be, modernist dances attract as much attention as the ballets termed classical, and the arguments against the latter have lost none of their force.

Fokine.—Every type of dance entertainment has its particular public and the attacks on ballet are not without reason. A ballet has no interest for me except there be created for each work steps and means of expression in accordance with the style of the theme. Many choregraphers have fallen into the old errors. No matter what the ballet the same system is always adopted : *pas de bourrée, entrechats,* always the feet turned out, and so on. It is nothing else but transporting to the stage the traditional exercises which every dancer performs daily. The greater part of the time, the choregraphy of a ballet is simply a more or less happy arrangement of exercises used in class.

An Enquirer after Knowledge.—Class exercises, but that is not choregraphy.

Fokine.—Certainly not ! Do not forget that we, on our side, are versed in the saltatory traditions of Perrot, Saint-Léon, Johannsen, and Petipa, and we have worked hard to perfect them still more. I cannot then be accused of heresy. The error, the fatal error, is the transportation of school exercises to the stage. The technique of the legs is insufficient, the whole body must work in harmony with the action—arms, hands, and features

A Professional.—But where is the actual danger ?

Fokine.—The danger is the stereotyped form of ballet, as I have just remarked. You have seen both the Greek myth of Prometheus and a Russian wedding interpreted with *pointes* and the most French of *pas de bourrée.* You cannot have failed to notice the artificiality and conventionality of such choregraphy. My reform was particularly directed to the preservation of style. Thus, in the " *Danse Hindoue* " in *Le Dieu Bleu,* the dancing is very *en dehors* ; in my Egyptian ballets the dancing is *en dedans* ; while in my Greek dances the positions of the feet are natural.

The Distinguished Man of Letters.—That seems logical to me. But why the deuce do not choregraphers always put this principle into practice ?

Fokine.—Because it is much easier to apply something one has always known, than continually to invent something new. Observe that the old ballet was not perfect, but beautiful, whereas the new ballet is often incomplete, but not at all beautiful.

The Misunderstood Poet.—The modern ballet ! How glorious ! Leonide Massine stated that ballets such as *Schéhérazade* and *Le Spectre de la Rose* were comparatively easy, while the apex of achievement, the culminating point, was *Le Sacre de Printemps.*

Fokine.—To which *Sacre de Printemps* are you referring ? Nijinsky's or Massine's ?

(The Misunderstood Poet does not reply).

Fokine.—My devil of a Petrouchka has been responsible for any number of natural children. The jerky movements of a doll have been introduced everywhere and on every possible occasion. It has become a habit. It is so easy to imitate Petrouchka's mechanical gestures. Neither choreographers nor dancers run any risk.

The Bibliophile.—And *Schéhérazade* ?

Fokine.—That is quite a different matter. *Schéhérazade* is the most onerous task for a choreographer. I have seen many reconstructions, even that of Massine, but all these attempts lacked something. There are groups and choreographic arrangements which in my ballet must explain the drama. There are neither conventional gestures nor conventional steps. It is one of the most difficult of ballets.

The Bibliophile.—And *Le Spectre de la Rose* ?

Fokine.—At the moment it is very difficult to find a dancer capable of filling that rôle as I conceived it, whereas it is quite easy to find executants for *Le Sacre de Printemps*, not only among professional dancers, but even among amateur dancers. In natural dancing, for most of the time, practically all the joints, numbering about two hundred, are in use, while in the doll dance the movements are mainly confined to one or two joints. Tell me, then, which of these two dances is the more difficult. I bid you good-day, Gentlemen.

APPENDIX B

RECEPTION OF FOKINE'S BALLETS BY THE LONDON PRESS

In general, beginning from 1911, the Diaghilev Company visited London immediately following the conclusion of their performances in Paris, and in order to show how Fokine's ballets were received by the London Press, typical notices from the most important periodicals are here set forth in chronological order.

1911 : SEASON AT ROYAL OPERA, COVENT GARDEN

LE PAVILLON D'ARMIDE

(First performed on the 21st of June)

" This little piece gives ample opportunity for some wonderfully expressive miming and in the scene of Armide and her Court for some varied dances of fresh and attractive character."—*Morning Post*, June 23rd.

LE CARNAVAL

(First performed on the 21st of June)

" The Schumann Carnaval was an unqualified joy from beginning to end, with never a moment when one felt that the music had been treated with anything but complete sympathy and understanding. . . . The entry of the Philistines was one of the great moments of the final number and the stage-management of the whole was among the most purely artistic the stage has ever seen."—*The Times*, June 22nd.

LE SPECTRE DE LA ROSE

(First performed on the 24th of June)

" The dream is a dream of perfect beauty and all too quickly over."—*Observer*, June 25th.

" A genuine poem, if ever one was portrayed on the stage."—*Daily Telegraph*, June 28th.

LES SYLPHIDES

(First performed on the 27th of June)

" Paderewski and Pachmann, when playing Chopin, have evoked visions of airy grace for us in stuffy concert-halls ; here we have the vision incarnate for us and breathed into fantastic life beneath the shadow of rocks and trees that belong only to the land of dreams."—*The Times*, July 8th.

" Beyond words, it is beautiful in its grace, its perfection of technique, its poetry, and its charms, and in the presentation of it."—*Daily Telegraph*, June 28th.

" Executed . . . with most charming effect, and the grace and delicacy of the soloists is informed by the elegant posse assumed the while by the *coryphées*."—*Morning Post*, June 28th.

CLÉOPÂTRE

(First performed on the 7th of July)

" The story matters little, being simply a peg on which to string a series of dances of exquisite beauty."—*The Times*, July 8th.

" It is no exaggeration to say that in the past twenty-five years its equal has not been seen in the same theatre."—*Daily Telegraph*, July 12th.

" The most interesting and attractive ballet given during the present season. . . . There is a series of delightful dances executed with new steps, new poses and new groupings."— *Morning Post*, July 8th.

SCHÉHÉRAZADE

(First performed on the 20th of July)

" There is a gorgeous savagery about the whole thing quite incommunicable in words, which are apt to give merely the impression of a violent piece of melodrama. That, however, is quite a secondary consideration ; the music, the movements, and the stage pictures all combine to carry one into a strange atmosphere in which life and death are nothing more than the expression of intense emotion, followed by its sudden cessation."—*The Times*, July 21st.

" From start to finish all was one stupendous orgie [*sic*] of sound and colour and movement, all in the most superb keeping."—*Daily Telegraph*, June 21st.

1912 : SEASON AT ROYAL OPERA, COVENT GARDEN

THAMAR
(First performed on the 12th of June)

" A bewildering series of dances ensues, each dance more picturesque than its predecessor, a veritable piling of Ossa on Pelion."—*Daily Telegraph*, June 13th.

" The groupings and pantomime of the Queen's attendants could not have been better."—*Observer*, June 16th.

" The piece is just one of those weird scenes of passion and colour—both rather crude—that the public expects from the Russian Ballet, and as such . . . meets with all approval."—*Morning Post*, June 13th.

L'OISEAU DE FEU
(First performed on the 18th of June)

" The stage picture as a whole was attractive with its brilliant, huddled, whirling masses centring round M. Bakst's superbly designed bird.

" Many of the dances are . . . finely conceived and carried out, and the colouring is splendidly bold and barbaric."—*The Times*, June 19th.

" It has provided the Russian Ballet with one of the finest displays of facility and proficiency in artistic miming that could possibly be conceived.

" The fascination of this ballet is the delightful way in which the dance associates itself with such inspiring material."—*Observer*, June 23rd.

" The most picturesque and bizarre of all the productions these wonderful Russians have yet shown us."—*Daily Telegraph*, June 21st.

" With the quaint theme, the quainter dresses, and the quaintest of all music the ballet is a complete novelty. Its figures of dance are altogether fresh, and the story seems to inspire all to better efforts than they have ever made before.

" The whole is an innovation that will attract all London, and will do so on merits that are entirely artistic."—*Morning Post*, June 19th.

NARCISSE
(First performed on the 9th of July)

" The grouping of the Boetian men and girls, the dances of the Bacchantes, and the unsullied joy of the first dances of

Narcissus . . . are as captivating as anything the Russians have given us."—*The Times*, July 10th.

" The whole thing is sheerly poetical."—*Observer*, July 14th.

" The ballet, full of rare poesy, is yet fantastic, and most picturesque. That its success was decided there is no doubt, for at the close of the one act of which the piece consists all and sundry connected with the performance were called and recalled many times."—*Daily Telegraph*, July 10th.

" There is a classic atmosphere in the story that is refreshing, and its execution shows the Russian dancers in a new light. The figures of the dances differ entirely from those already seen, and there is greater charm, more grace, and less suggestion of the acrobatic.

" The whole production is calculated to win a new reputation for the Russian ballet. It is the means of placing its art on a higher level and should be the medium for widening its circle of admirers."—*Morning Post*, July 10th.

1913 : SEASON AT ROYAL OPERA, COVENT GARDEN

PETROUCHKA

(First performed on the 4th of February)

" It is all horribly macabre and extraordinarily effective. There are a few dull moments in the Moor's show box and one expects a longer glimpse of the puppets before the final scuffle, but the whole thing is refreshingly new and refreshingly Russian, more Russian, in fact, than any ballet we have had.—*The Times*, February 5th.

" It is supremely clever, supremely modern and supremly, baroque."—*Observer*, February 9th.

" A most fascinating work, alike delightful in its staging and its music. . . . The colour scheme on the stage and the grouping and arranging of the dancers was as exquisite as ever."—*Daily Chronicle*, February 5th.

LE DIEU BLEU

(First performed on the 27th of February)

" Every advantage is taken of the opportunity for quaint design and colour, and many of the dresses are magnificent."—*Morning Post*, February 28th.

LE COQ D'OR
(First performed on the 15th of June)

" A riot of gorgeous colour, a wealth of skilful music, absurdities which brought roars of laughter even without understanding of the witty text which was being sung all the time, its only fault was that so much necessarily passed unnoticed, and with so much to see it was difficult to keep the ears alert."—*The Times*, June 16th.

" Certainly it is a feast for the eye—a mass of superb colour effects, ever varying with the artistically arranged movement of the chorus garbed in sumptuous, flaunting raiment, with every turn providing a coup de théâtre."—*Observer*, June 28th.

" We have said that this is a thing to see and not to write of. It is an entertainment of the most amusing character for those that have a laugh left in them, and it is inconceivable that anything, serious or other, could be more gorgeously presented or more beautifully performed . . . the quite extraordinary unison of the choregraphs [*sic*] and their vocal counterparts, all this—and much more—raised last night's performance to a level undreamt of here before."—*Daily Telegraph*, June 16th.

LA LÉGENDE DE JOSEPH
(First performed on the 23rd of June)

" There are some beautiful conceptions in united movement, notably in the processions, the dances of the veiled and unveiled women and the bewildering and curious boxers' dances, and, most satisfactory of all, the wonderful fantastic dance of the women of the Palace, when they treat Joseph, after his refusal to yield to the proposal of Potiphar's wife, as an evil spirit. There are many things in *Joseph* that should prove extraordinarily attractive, but they are not concerned with the music, fine as it is, or the book. They are due to the artistic resource of M. Fokine, M. Bakst, a marvellous troupe of exponents of their particular ideas, and M. Jose Maria Serb [*sic*], whose scenery is highly effective."—*Observer*, June 28th.

" It is truly a wonderful thing, the new ballet, wonderful even in this day, when the Russians are piling up wonders, each new production seeming to surpass in richness and splendour all that had preceded it. Whether one regards it from the philosophical standpoint, or merely the pictorial, it is equally ' sensational ' in its amazing effect . . . the most sumptuous of the Russian ballets has not shown us a greater glory, a finer

riot of brilliant colour, mauves, greens, blues, mingling with each other in wildest profusion, yet never is a false note struck."
—*Daily Telegraph*, June 24th.

1914: SEASON AT THEATRE ROYAL, DRURY LANE

DAPHNIS ET CHLOÉ
(First performed on the 9th of June)

" It is an idyll in which the stage pictures of Chloë carried away by robbers, of her recovery by the intervention of Pan at the prayer of Daphnis, and of their miming together the story of the love of Pan and Syrinx have served to stimulate the composer's imagination, and now act primarily as the link which puts the imagination of the hearers into contact with the spirit of the music. This does not mean that the action is unimportant, but that the beauty of the scenes, the poses of the groups of Grecian figures, the dances alike of the individuals, the masses of youths and maidens, and of the pirates, seem to take their places in the scheme primarily as illustrations of the symphonic poem played by the orchestra."—*The Times*, June 10th.

" The stage pictures attached to the progress of the ballet are highly poetical, and the dances are wonderfully conceived."
—*Observer*, June 14th.

" The first of the new numbers is certainly most successful. It is a choregraphic version of the classic Daphnis et Chloë, but unlike the new pieces the Ballet gave last season, it has the advantage of being thoroughly artistic. There is none of the weird posturing that was inflicted on us last year; in its place there is remarkably graceful and legitimate dancing, elegant posing, and most effective grouping. The old story serves well, and with the aid of . . . well designed figures of dance is turned into a most pleasing ballet."—*Morning Post*, June 10th.

" The grouping of the figures, the dances, and the costumes have all been done with that consummate art one has now come to expect from these Russian artists. There are many pictures to delight the eye, especially the two scenes in the sacred grove."—*Daily Chronicle*, June 10th.

PAPILLONS
(First performed on the 11th of June)

" *Papillons* . . . is a pretty, picturesque little story . . . adapted very effectively to the progress of the music. It is a fitting pendant to the delightful *Carnaval.*"—*Observer*, June 21st.

" It is all very pleasing, creating much the same fragrant charm as *Carnaval*, but on a smaller scale."—*Morning Post*, June 12th.

" The dances, which are more upon classical lines than in the modernised style of most Russian ballets, are quite charming, and the *pas seuls* for the young girl who coquets with Pierrot, and the *pas de deux* which they dance together are exquisitely dainty and charming, and characteristic of M. Fokine's genius for effect."—*Daily Chronicle*, June 12th.

APPENDIX C

SUMMARY OF THE ACTIVITIES OF MICHEL FOKINE

During the Period 1918–1931.

Including Performances given by Vera Fokina

Note.—* New version of a former composition; ** first performance in any country; *** first performance in any country and an important work.

1918

March   7th and 11th at Abo, Finland.
             25th and 27th at Opera Royal, Stockholm, Sweden.
April   2nd and 4th at Göteborg, Sweden.
             11th at Malmö, Sweden.
             16th at Helsingborg, Sweden.
             21st at Kristianstad, Sweden.
             22nd at Lund, Sweden.
             26th at Landkrona, Sweden.
             28th at Ystad, Sweden.
             29th at Malmö, Sweden.
May   2nd, 4th, and 7th at Royal Opera, Stockholm.
             6th at Dramatic Theatre, Stockholm.
             8th at Norrköping, Sweden.
             12th and 14th at King's Theatre, Copenhagen, Denmark.
             21st, 23rd, 27th, 29th and 31st, at the New Theatre, Copenhagen.
June, July, August.   Teaching at Helsingör, Denmark.
September   21st, Production at the Stockholm Stadium in celebration of the "Barnens Day," with 800 girls taking part, of the *Four Seasons*.***
             22nd, at the same Stadium with the same participants, production of Beethoven's "Moonlight Sonata."
November   22nd, at the Casino, Copenhagen, Denmark.
December   15th, Mme. Fokina *alone* at the Odd-Fellow Palace, Copenhagen.

1919

January 1st, Göteborg, Sweden.
28th, National Theatre, Kristiania, (Oslo), Norway.
February 2nd, Kristiania, Norway, Mme. Vera Fokina *alone*.
6th, 8th, 9th, Trondhjem, Mme. Vera Fokina *alone*.
12th, National Theatre, Kristiania, Mme. Vera Fokina *alone*.
24th and 26th, Bergen, Mme. Vera Fokina *alone*.
March 1st, 3rd, 6th, Stavanger, Mme. Vera F kina *alone*.
10th, Uddevalla, Mme. Vera Fokina *alone*.
11th, Slogelse, Mme. Vera Fokina *alone*.
May 10th, 12th, 15th, 18th, at Royal Opera, Stockholm. (both Michel and Vera Fokine).
June, July, August, September, teaching at Charlotenlund, Denmark.
December 1st, Production of dances in *Aphrodite*,*** Century Theatre, New York City, U.S.A.
30th performance of M. and V. Fokine at the Metropolitan Opera House, New York City.

1920

January 18th at the New York Hippodrome, N.Y.C.
19th at Boston, Mass.
February 10th at Metropolitan Opera House, N.Y.C., Mme. Fokina *alone*.
26th at Washington D.C., Mme. Fokina *alone*.
March 22nd at Metropolitan Opera House, Philadelphia, Penn., Mme. Fokina *alone*.
May 1st, at Metropolitan Opera House, N.Y.C.
29th, at New York Hippodrome, N.Y.C.
October 4th, production of Dances in *Mecca**, Century Theatre, N.Y.C.
22nd, Syracuse, N.Y.
25th, Pittsburg, Penn.
28th, Wheeling, Penn.
31st, Dayton, Ohio.
November 4th, Sagnow.
Other performances of M. and V. Fokine in U.S.A. in 1920 include Auditorium Theatre, Chicago, Ann Arbor, Grand Rapids, Philadelphia, etc. (dates not available).

1921

January 1st, Opening of the FOKINE SCHOOL in New York City.

19th, Symphony Hall, Boston, Mass.

24th, Academy of Music, Philadelphia, Penn. Mme. Fokina *alone* performed the " Four Periods of the Ballet " at the Academy of Music Anniversary Ball.

February 21st, production of the ballet in *Rose Girls***, N.Y.C.

March 1st, Metropolitan Opera House, N.Y.C., performance with *Le Rêve de la Marquise*.***

May 11th and 30th, *Soirée de Danses* of M. and V. Fokine, at the Grand Opera, Paris.

June 4th, same as above.

20th, 22nd, 24th, 27th, performances of the ballet *Daphnis et Chloé**, with French artists and personal appearances of M. and V. Fokine in the leading rôles. At the Grand Opera, Paris.

September 3rd, production of *The Thunder Bird****, at the New York Hippodrome, starting on the 3rd of Sept., 1921. This ballet ran for 20 consecutive weeks, the first 10 weeks were with daily personal appearances of M. and V. Fokine in the leading rôles.

October 3rd, production of *The Shaytan's Captive*,** music by Glazunov (from " Raymonda ") for Gertrude Hoffman Co., at the Palace Theatre, N.Y.C.

Production of *Russian Toys*** ballet for Gilda Gray and her company (no date), N.Y.C.

1922

February (No dates), performances of M. and V. Fokine in Roanok, Richmond, Norfolk, Philadelphia, Boston, etc.

October 15th, Mark Strand Theatre, N.Y.C., Fokine Ballet there for 10 weeks, company consisted of pupils from Studio. Productions given—*Adventures of Harlequin****, *Voices of Spring*,** (Strauss), *Chinese Dance*, (Rebikov), *Russian Toys**, and so on.

December 25th, Central Theatre, N.Y.C., production for Gertrude Hoffman Co. :—*Russian Dance Scene*,* (Rubinstein), *Apache Dance Scene**, *Les Sylphides**, Waltz *Blue Danube*.*

1923

January	1st, *The Dying Swan, Gipsy Dance*, Stanley Theatre, Philadelphia, Penn., Mme. Fokina.

8th, Stanley Theatre, Philadelphia, Penn. Mme. Fokina for one week, *The Thunder Bird, Russian Dance*.

29th, production of the ballet in the play *Johannes Kreisler*, Apollo Theatre, N.Y.C.

March   Lectures by Michel Fokine on the subject of Ballet at the Al Jolson Theatre, N.Y.C.

April   23rd, production for Ziegfeld Follies at the New Amsterdam Theatre, N.Y.C., of *Farljandio***, by J. Reynolds, music by Victor Herbert, and *Frolicking Gods****, by Michel Fokine, both staged by Michel Fokine.

September   20th, production of dances in *Hassan*** at His Majesty's Theatre, London, England.

26th, Production of dances for prologue *The Return from the Carnival****, for the play " *Casanova*," at the Empire Theatre, N.Y.C.; being in England at the time, Fokine was not present at the first performance.

Santa Claus,* ballet to the music of Lyadov, produced for G. Hoffman Co., Newark, N.J., (no date).

Dances in *The Miracle*,** Century Theatre, N.Y.C., music by Humperdinck.

1924

January   7th, *Spanish Ballets* (*Sevilla** and *Seguidilla**), music by Albeniz, at Monday Opera Supper Club, participants were society ladies (charity performance).

February   26th, Michel Fokine and Vera Fokine and their American ballet, at the Metropolitan Opera House, N.Y.C. :—

         I. Ballet *Elves*, *music by Mendelssohn.

         II. *The Dying Swan*.*

         III. *Medusa*,*** Symphonie Pathétique by Tchaikovsky.

         IV. *Le Rêve de la Marquise** (Mozart).

         V. *Antique Frieze* (Glazunov), (dance for three girls).

         VI. *Ole Toro*,** Capriccio Espagnole by Rimsky-Korsakov.

163

April   14th, one week, *The Shemakhanskaya Tsaritsa,*** (Rimsky-Korsakov), Mme. Fokina and the Fokine dancers at the Stanley Theatre, Philadelphia.

Auguſt   8th, produ&tion of the *Oriental Ballet,*** (Ippolitov-Ivanov) Charity Ball at Asbury Park, N.J. (participants were society ladies).

May   30th, The Fokine Dancers in a dance programme. Sleepy Hollow Country Club, N.Y.

September   22nd, dances in *Hassan,*** Knickerbocker Theatre, N.Y.C.

1925

February   16th, produ&tion of *The Immortal Pierrot,**** with the Fokine Dancers at the 81ſt Street Theatre, N.Y.C.

March   9th, *Frolicking Gods,** at Liverpool, England, later same produ&tion at the London Hippodrome (no date).

April   *European Tour of M. and V. Fokine,* including ballets *Fra Mina* (Schumann : Sinfonischen Etudes).

24th, 25th, 26th, 27th, Lessing Theatre, Berlin, Germany.

30th, New Theatre, Copenhagen, Denmark.

May   2nd, 5th, 7th, New Theatre, Copenhagen, Denmark.

13th, Finska Theatre, Helsingfors, Finland.

15th, Eſtonia Theatre, Revel, Eſtonia.

18th and 19th, National Opera, Riga, Latvia.

20th, Finska Theatre, Helsingfors, Finland.

26th and 28th, King's Theatre, Stockholm, Sweden.

June   2nd, Hippodrome, Malmö, Sweden.

4th, Helsingborg Theatre, Helsingborg.

6th, Hippodrome, Malmö.

October   21ſt, Produ&tion of *Petrouchka,** *Les Sylphides,** and Polovtsian Dances from *Prince Igor,* at King's Theatre, Copenhagen, Denmark.

1926

February   27th, Mme. Fokina in a performance at the Carnegie Hall, N.Y.C., all dances created and arranged by M. Fokine. Fokine Ballet in *Venetian Carnival,*[1] and *Caucasian Sketches,*[2] (Oriental Ballet), Club Mirador, N.Y.C. (no date).

[1] New Version of *The Return from the Carnival.*
[2] New Version of *Oriental Ballet.*

May   3rd, for one week, Mme. Vera Fokina and the Fokine Ballet in *The Mountain Queen*,[1] (Ippolitov-Ivanov and Rimsky-Korsakov), at Keith-Albee Theatre, N.Y.C., Mosque Theatre, Newark; Boston, Mass., etc. (no dates).

December   4th, Lecture and dances at Whitehall Club, N.Y.C.

1927

February   7th to 21st, Mme. Fokina and Fokine Girls at Stanley Theatre, Philadelphia, Penn., in *Faust* ballet,** (Prologue to *Faust*).

        13th, Lecture on Dances at the affair of the Russian National University, N.Y.C.

November   10th and 11th, Masonic Auditorium, Detroit, M. and V. Fokine and the Fokine Ballet.

        Lewisohn Stadium, N.Y.C., 3 performances of Michel and Vera Fokine and their Ballet, numbers included *Elves*, *Medusa*, and *divertissement*. (Forty-eight thousand people in audience for 3 performances) (summer—no date).

        Century Theatre, N.Y.C., M. and V. Fokine and Fokine Ballet including *Elves*, *Cléopâtre*,* and a *divertissement*, 4 performances (no dates).

        M. and V. Fokine and Fokine Ballet in Cleveland, Ohio (no date).

1928

January   10th, Production of *The Ballet of Flowers*,** in the musical comedy *Rosalie*, a Ziegfeld production at the New Amsterdam Theatre, N.Y.C.

May   28th, Production of the *South Sea Island Dance*,** at the Booth Theatre, N.Y.C., for the Grand Street Follies.

1929

January   26th or 27th? Production of Polovtsian Dances from *Prince Igor*,* in Théâtre des Champs Elysées, for Opéra Privé de Paris.

February   7th and 8th, Production of the Polovtsian Dances from *Prince Igor*, also *Les Sylphides*, for the National Opera, Riga, Latvia. With personal appearances of M. Fokine in leading rôles.

[1] New Version of *Shemakhanskaya Tsaritsa* and *Oriental Ballet*.

April	28th. Composition of dances (9 new) for the performance of Mme. Anna Robenne at her recital in John Golden Theatre, N.Y.C.
July	From 8th, Master Class of the Dance, in Hollywood, California.
August	9th, Performance at Hollywood Bowl, Hollywood, of M. and V. Fokine in a programme of dances, with symphony orchestra.
	16th, Hollywood Bowl, *Bacchanale,** from *Tannhäuser*, with Mme. Fokina and Mr. Fokine's Californian pupils.

1930

There is little to record for this year. The impresario, Morris Gest, discussed with Fokine a plan for the organisation of a School of Ballet, and the production of Fokine's ballets and their filming for kinematographic representation. As a result of their conversation, Fokine closed his school. But when he returned from Hollywood to New York, he found that Mr. Gest had been taken ill and consequently it was not possible to proceed with the scheme agreed upon.

Fokine then drove in his car back to Hollywood, where a new disappointment awaited him. The magnates of the film world pronounced his work to be too serious and told him that he was too artistic! Fokine then returned to New York where he re-established his school.

1931

June to November	Produced at the Colon Theatre, Buenos Aires, Argentine, *Schéhérazade, Les Sylphides, Polovtsian Dances from Prince Igor, L'Oiseau de Feu, Le Spectre de la Rose, Le Carnaval,* and entirely new versions of *The Adventures of Harlequin* and *The Sorcerer's Pupil* (*L'Apprenti Sorcier*).

The original *Adventures of Harlequin*, produced at New York in 1922, with 11 dancers, played for 10 minutes. The new version had 100 dancers and lasted 25 minutes.

The new version of *The Sorcerer's Pupil*, originally produced at St. Petersburg in 1916, had the water dance given on a revolving stage. This was an entirely new development of stage technique, and by this means the " water " flowed into the room and then flowed away. Some very interesting effects were produced by the contrasting dances presented simultaneously on the static and revolving stages.

INDEX

167